Project North Africa's First Year of
Ministry to Muslims

Ramblings from North Africa

Project North Africa

ISBN: 978-1-932963-01-4

Printed in the United States by:
Morris Publishing
3212 East Highway 30
Kearney, NE 68847
1-800-650-7888

To our mentors and pastors:

Pastor Roger Green, Grace Baptist Church, Middletown, OH.
Pastor Austin Gardner, Vision Baptist Church, Alpharetta, GA.
Pastors Steve and Josh Grubbs, Shenandoah Baptist Church,
Shenandoah, TN.
Missionary Pastor Chris Gardner, Faith Baptist Church, Arequipa,
Peru.

...because you modeled and taught us that II Tim. 2:2 is a global
principle.

"And the things which thou hast heard of me, among many
witnesses, the same commit them to faithful men who shall be able
to teach others also." II Tim 2:2

Contents

Foreword

Our hearts beat with I. Trotter, Missionary to Algeria, who said over 100 years ago, "We who have loved them see the possibilities of sacrifice, of endurance, of enthusiasm of life, not yet effaced. Does not the Son of God who died for them see these possibilities, too? Do you think He says of the Muslim, 'There is no help for him in God'?"

My wife and I, along with Cesar and his wife Mariet, our coworkers from Peru, have put in this book over 100 individual experiences during 2007, our first year working with and living amongst Muslims. The topics include our anticipation and fear prior to departure, our observances of the Muslim practices, testimonies of new believers in Christ, and pretty much anything we experienced that we thought could be of a help to someone with a heart for Muslims. We have not printed this book to praise ourselves. On the contrary, our mistakes have far outweighed our successes, of which, all the praise belongs to God. Rather we have printed this book because of Christ's love for the Muslim people of the Maghreb and our failure to plant churches here. The Maghreb is a block of five countries including: Mauritania, Morocco, Libya, Algeria, and Tunisia with a combined population of over 100 million people.

Maybe the reason for the lack of laborers is because our churches have not seen the possibilities of God's glory here in Muslim countries. Maybe it's because we lacked the patience and the courage to plant, water, and reap amongst people so traditionally resistant to the gospel. Maybe it's because we just have never heard of cities of millions with less than a handful of believers. Maybe it's because we don't know how to plant churches where we cannot put up a sign and drive through the streets with a loud speaker. Whatever the reason, we hope this book of our experiences here will motivate you to pray and send laborers.

We have not included the name of the specific country and city that we are working in. The reason for this is out of respect of some of the national believers that we worked with this last year. Some believers are more bold and don't mind who knows. Do not, however, get the idea that we are in extreme danger because of this. A friend of mine on a recent trip once told his congregation that "we are risking our lives" to be here. That is no more true than of missionaries in most any other part of the world from South America to Europe. There is a possibility that we will be kicked out of the country but the risk of physical injury is very small. There are missionaries in countries like Afghanistan, Pakistan, Saudi Arabia, parts of Indonesia, and a handful of other countries who are in serious risk. It would be unfair to them for anyone to believe the same about us. Our hope is that you will read this book and see all the possibilities for ministry though ministry for Christ here is technically against the laws of men.

So why did we print this book?

-To spread the word of the great need and opportunity in the Muslim world. We hope many will answer the Christ's call to "GO". We have included testimonies of more than twenty-five ex-Muslims so you can be encouraged at what God is doing to redeem Muslims in the darkest corners of the world.

-To bridge the gap of understanding between the church and the missionary. We want you to know what life is like ministering in a Muslim country. With understanding comes a more informed and concerted effort of prayer back home.

-To take the mystery out of ministering to Muslims. It can be done by normal people.

-To give the churches boldness. Our passion is to boldly preach the name of Christ to the entire Muslim world. They won't take the gospel seriously until we stop hiding from their threats and laws.

What this book is not:

-This book is not a doctrinal thesis on Islam and the teachings of the Koran. We do not approach ministry to Muslims theoretically but practically. We try to understand what the average Muslim, our friends, believe. That is often very different from what Islam actually teaches.

-This book is not a "How To" on missions to Muslims. We hope this book will give you ideas if you are ministering to Muslims but to think that you should do what we have done would be error. We have made many, many mistakes and have yet to prove an effective way to plant churches in Muslim cities. One reason I didn't want to print this book is the criticism we will undoubtedly receive for how we haven't done ministry right. We know that and admit it readily. If we have done anything unbiblical, we will change. For those methods we employ that are biblical we make no apology.

-This book is not written by scholars. These are merely notes we have taken as envision churches being planted all over North Africa. We have been tempted to change many things to make us look better where we made mistakes or make our language sound more scholarly but we decided to just print it as it was written. Since these are journal entries they would lose their character if we had done so.

-Most of all, this book is not to praise the authors. We want Christ to receive the glory in North Africa and through our lives.

For whom did we write this book?

-For future missionaries (whether you know it yet or not) who will be helped by knowing some of our struggles and victories, mistakes and successes. I wish I could have known what things we would likely face before arriving.

-For Pastors who send their young people to Muslim fields. The Pastor has the charge to lead his people into the battlefields and support with understanding those sent ones.

-The layman who is passionate about missions. We hope you find that we are just normal people like you who are privileged to work in missions full time.

-For college students who are praying about what God wants them to do with their lives and where he wants them to do that. We hope your heart will break like ours for the 1.3 billion Muslims. They are the greatest challenge to missions today.

-For our supporters who we want to thank for your love, prayers, and financial gifts to allow us to live out Christ's love for Muslims. We hope you can know us personally and our joint mission better through this book.

-Aaron

The Scene

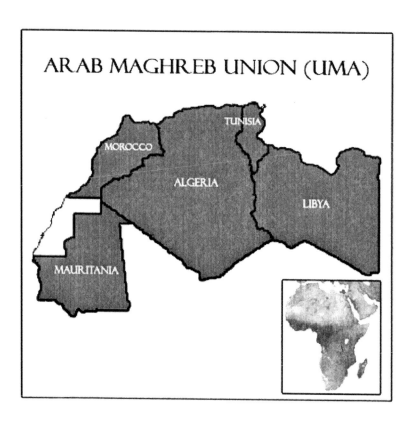

The Maghreb- Population 2006

99% Muslim

Morocco	34,241,259
Algeria	32,930,091
Tunisia	10,175,014
Libya	5,900,754
Mauritania	3,177,388

The country we stepped into is one of great beauty as we discovered. Beautiful snow covered mountains, green pastures, immense deserts, long stretches of sun-drenched beaches, not what you might expect to find in Africa. It is a contrast of riches and poverty, secularism and Islamic fundamentalism, modern and traditional. Most Muslim countries have one foot in 700 A.D. and one foot in 2007.

It is also a place that has been long resistant to the gospel. Since the Muslims invaded in 700 A.D. the whole of Africa north of the Sahara desert has been Muslim. Thankfully the Sahara stopped the advance of the Muslim soldiers in that time, though today it is moving with lightning quick speed into central Africa. The first missionary came to North Africa in the 13th century. He was a catholic priest named Robert Lull who determined to use Christ's love on the Muslims and not the sword of the crusader. He saw a handful of converts and eventually was martyred.

There are no other missionaries on record from his time until the time of the Student Volunteer Missionary Movement in the late 1800's and then it was mostly women. Samuel Zwimmer came here and sold Bibles during the time of the French occupation. There was a freedom of religion when the French ruled all of the Maghreb except for Libya. Today that freedom has been abolished for more than 60 years.

Though it is against the law to "shake the faith of a Muslim" we hope you will see just how possible it is to work here. We have not yet found the limit to ministry. I am sure some day we will. Our country thrives on tourism, so in turn, it loves foreigners. There are less than 3,000 professing believers in Jesus Christ in our country. That is less than a tenth of a percent of the population. The encouraging news is that just ten years ago there were only around 300 believers. So that number has multiplied ten times in ten years. If we saw that kind of growth in America, we would have no one left to evangelize.

The cause for this growth has been largely due to mass media evangelism like Satellite TV, radio, and Internet. The great lack is training and churches. Many new believers in Christ are left without a church, a Bible, or a pastor. Our passion is to remedy that.

My wife and I launched a dream that we call Project North Africa along with Tyler and Gretchen Masters under Macedonia World Baptist Missions in January 2006. It is a dream to mobilize church planters to the Muslim world starting in North Africa. It is a dream to reach millions of Muslims with the gospel of Jesus Christ through mass media. It is a dream to disciple Muslim Background Believers into men and women of God.

Our dream hit the ground in January of 2007 with our arrival on the soil of North Africa and February 2007 with the arrival of our first Latin couple, Cesar and Mariet. We have been working since that time to learn their language, culture, and religion. Like most dreams it came close to dying in my heart around the months of April, May, and June. As God taught us to trust in Him he began to show us his power. This book is our personal thoughts and experiences in that setting.

January
From Aaron's Personal Journal

Jan 7

We are leaving for North Africa in 6 days. Huge move. I am beginning to get a bit nervous. Jillian, though, is doing great. She has a great attitude and is showing herself to be a real God-called woman. It is awesome to have such a beautiful, personable, sweet, and godly woman as my helpmeet. My prayer is that many young women would be able to mimic her passion and heart.

Jan 10

When I think about the immense job before us I shrivel. I question my desires. Are they God-motivated or self-motivated? Do I want to plant churches in Muslim cities for my name's sake or is it that the almighty God is planning on using me to perform that task? I must say, Lord, I don't know exactly how you will lead me or what you will use me to accomplish but just help me, like Andrew, not to desire greatness for myself but for your name.

Jan 12

I remember about 13 months ago in December of 2005. I had returned from my trip to Egypt where I was hoping God would give me some sort of epiphany about the future of my ministry. I was staying at Jeff Andrew's house in Arequipa, Peru with my little family. It was a large, strange home that fit my fears perfectly. Three pastors from America who are my three biggest financial supporters stayed with us for one week. I never felt so alone in my life. I didn't understand the future of "Project North Africa" that was in its seed stage yet I had to sell these men on it. I faced uncertainty but not with joy. My stomach was eaten up on the inside. I was full of fears. For the next three months or so I wanted to die because I didn't know what God was going to do next. He hadn't mapped it all out for me yet.

Now it is one year later. I could've never imagined then what God would do in 2006 or where we would invest 2007. The future is still uncertain. On the eve of our departure through it all, I have learned to trust in you, to rest in you. I have more reason now to feel alone than I did then but my stomach feels fine. I am not afraid. I am not anxious. By the grace of God. I have learned, Lord, that my greatest fears will not be realized, my worrying is vain, the possibilities of the future are much brighter than they are dark, that my greatest and only necessary fan is you, and that at the end of the day I will win. My wife will love and appreciate me, my kids will respect and honor me, my supporters will be few but loyal, and my fruit will be harvested in it's season.

Just help me, Lord to not be moved by doubtful supporters or an uphill climb. Though all those weigh against me, let me stand. I will win in Jesus Christ, which strengtheneth me.

February

We arrived about three weeks ago. In that time we have found a house to rent and got everything set up. Our house is on the 5th floor of an eighth story building. Almost everyone lives in apartments like this. Ours has a beautiful view of part of the city. This city is around 1.5 million people. I stepped out on our balcony our first night in the new place and was engulfed with the sound of the call to prayer in the nearby mosque. My heart broke for these people without light and I thanked God for bringing me here to be that light. As we prepared to come to North Africa I was always excited to meet the occasional Muslim in Atlanta as I tried to witness to them.

We thank the Lord that before we came we were able to see around 40 of them visit the church we were working in, Vision Baptist Church in Alpharetta, GA. One of them even accepted Christ as her Savior. Her name is Shayma. She is from a Kurdish town in Iraq on the border of Turkey. She accepted Christ as a result of an older lady who loved her and shared the Word. Right after Shayma had arrived in the States with her family, she spoke no English. After school this older lady was their next-door neighbor and would invite her over for cookies after school. While Shayma ate the cookies the lady would read the Bible to her. Shayma didn't understand much because she didn't understand the English but she caught the love that was in that ladies heart. After about 2 months of coming to our church she bowed her head and accepted Christ with my wife. She said that she had always wanted to be a Christian ever since she met that lady but didn't know how. Experiences like that before we came here to the field give irreplaceable hope for this country. I would recommend that no one go to a Muslim field until they have worked with some of the 7 million Muslims in the US.

I went to the capital to pick up a container about half full of all of our belongings yesterday. It took me one full day running in and out of the port following a North African man who walked faster than I can run all around the port signing one paper after another while sliding five or ten bucks to whoever required it under the table. After getting our container out of the port and through a brief customs check, which consisted of him asking me if I have anything illegal in the container, we had to unload our stuff into a truck. Then I rode in the front of the truth with three men. One was a 21-year-old kid named Amine. I could say much but we practiced for five straight hours all I could say.

We said "I, you, he, she, they, we" about 100 times in Arabic. They taught me all the colors, practiced the numbers one through twenty. I am trying to commit one verb to memory each day I am here. I am at about 15 verbs now so I completely exhausted those pretty quickly. Anyway, after arriving in our city I passed Amine a New Testament as a gift as we exchanged phone numbers. I don't know if I'll ever have a chance to explain the love of Christ to him in Arabic, but I dream of that day.

After three weeks we are reading and writing the Arabic script. I don't have any idea what it says yet but I can painstakingly read. I have started to read my Bible in Arabic. The first day I started with John chapter 1 verse 1. The first verse took me over an hour. ONE VERSE! I hope it gets better or we are going to have some pretty long Bible studies in the future. Everywhere I go I read. I read billboards, labels on cans at the super market, flyers, business signs, everything. My wife is afraid that people are going to think I am crazy. Everywhere I go I am always looking up and mumbling to myself. I am sure that I'm not pronouncing it right but it helps to recognize all the letters.

Having no church

The hardest thing about our first month here has been having no church. It has literally been the most potentially discouraging thing I have ever been through. We have fought hard to not let it discourage us but it gets to you. There are about ten missionary families in this city. Few of them meet with the national church. They all warn us to not meet with the churches as it puts them in danger with the presence of a foreigner. It is no wonder they are all so discouraged in their ministry.

The whole country of 33 million people has around 30 house churches. The city we are in has two. One meets once a month or so and the other one meets weekly. The one runs maybe fifteen and the other around ten. I have asked and practically begged the Americans connected with the smaller house church to let us be involved. They always give us a patronizing look and tell us we can come later after we have been here a while. It reminds me of when my parents used to tell me of all the stuff I could do "once you grow up". The second group was warned by the first of these "dangerous" Americans who pass out Bibles and talk about Jesus too much so they won't let us attend either. I have to remember that when people do that they are not rejecting me, they are rejecting Him that sent me.

So what do we do? Jillian and I get together and try to hold the kids quiet. I tried leading singing once but we quickly changed the program of the service when I couldn't get my congregation to join me! We pray, read some of the Bible, talk about what God is doing in our hearts, and then I share with her a message that I prepared before we came here just for this occasion. I try to go easy on the invitation so I don't make my congregation feel uncomfortable! I have to constantly remind myself that it is because of this very hardship we need to be here. There are no brave churches meeting to get the gospel to these people! We want the Lord to use us to see that that doesn't stay that way.

March

On February 22nd Cesar and his wife Miriam arrived. God worked out a miracle in the airport to get them in the country. It is a huge blessing to have them here, as I am not the only one to preach anymore. No missionary should come to a field like this alone if at all possible. We are working on language school together now and we're trying to help them catch up.

Soon after Cesar arrived I got hold of the phone number of a national pastor in a city about an hour from here. I was dying to be part of a national church since that is the only reason we are here, so I called him. I introduced myself to him and was fortunate that he speaks enough Spanish to understand me since my Arabic isn't ready for phone conversations. I asked if we could meet him on Sunday "since we'd be in his town". Truth was the only reason I was going to be in his town was to meet him and Sunday because I wanted him to invite us to come to his church. I had learned from experience not to ask that directly. So as soon as I told him I'd be in his town on Sunday he said, "Oh, we have a meeting with the church on Sunday. You can just come to that." He was surprised by my enthusiastic response; "I have two kids and another family with me. No problem?" "Of course not. Bring them all." He confirmed. I was thrilled.

On Sunday we took the hour-long taxi ride and waited at the taxi stop for him to come pick us up. He showed up in the van of an American missionary. Thankfully, this American wasn't like all the others we had met. First thing he told me when we piled all six of us into his van was, "You can't learn language and ministry without being part of a church every week." I almost kissed him. We haven't missed a Sunday there at that church unless we were out of the country since that Sunday. Sometimes they have had up to 30 and once it was just my family, Cesar's family, and one other man but we were thrilled.

I have made it a point of not going to the International Church that the other missionaries attend. Really it is just a meeting for the missionaries. You will find that repeated all over the Muslim world.

In every city there will be a church typically in English that only foreigners are allowed to go to. It is inevitably full of missionaries who are wasting their own time and a lot of the churches' money because they are afraid to plant a national church. Anyone who attends there will be brought down by the influence of those who attend. We have to learn to sing, pray, and preach in Arabic.

April

I have been super excited this month because of a young man named Ali. A few American college students who are here in the city had been witnessing to him. Together we started doing some Bible studies in English. Since he worked with tourists for a long time he speaks very well. For about four weeks he was right there with us. He was giving New Testaments to his friends and inviting them to come along. A few even did. A national believer was helping us out in Arabic with all the difficult things that Muslims struggle with. Ali had questions mostly about the Trinity and the veracity of the Bible. One night we studied what it means to be born again. He seemed excited as he said he finally understands how he can be a Christian. He said a prayer and accepted Christ! I was sending emails, put it in my prayer letter, making phone calls…I was excited!

As excited as I had become was only equaled by the discouragement that followed when it became obvious that he had been with us and made a profession of faith just so he could get money. He has asked me twice for large amounts of money and when I don't give it to him I can see him gradually losing interest in our Bible studies. Now I have stopped inviting him because he can never make it when he always had time before.

Some of the missionaries here have used this type of thing as a reason not to witness to people. They say that the people will only listen for money. So their solution is to make friends with people, hook them up with a national believer, and little by little the national believer can tell them about Christ. One national Christian even warned me about blood sucking nationals and told me to just let them (the national believers) do the job. Now that all sounds great in your indigenous philosophy but lets do the math…

1,500,000   # of people in the city

Divided by

5   # of mature national men who are believers in Christ capable of opening the Bible and showing someone how to be saved

=300,000   # of people that each national believer needs to witness to and disciple.

Now, I am not a genius but even if we multiplied the believers by ten just to be safe, there is no way we'll reach all these people with the gospel that way. I guess we'll just keep doing what Jesus told us to and let the chips fall where they may. I think I remember a few thousand people coming to eat fish and chips with Jesus who were nowhere to be found when he was crucified. Miracles and free food always bring the crowds out. That's not a bad thing as long as we ask God to help us find those who are serious out of the crowd.

The Platform

We are starting a business this month in order to get Cesar and his wife their residency papers. I guess I should say this year we are starting a business. Just the paperwork to have the business legit has taken almost two months even after paying $1,000 to pay a man whose job it is to do all the paperwork for new companies. Our business is a language school. We are going to teach Spanish and English to North Africans and Arabic to foreigners who visit us. Since everyone here wants to learn one of those two, it shouldn't be too hard to drum up students for the ten American college students who will be here this summer. This business, or platform, is not our real reason for being here but gives us a reason to be here with the government.

These businesses are why many people call these "closed" countries, "creative access" countries. Many books have been written on starting businesses in closed countries. Many students I meet in Bible colleges are studying different professions to get access to countries like this. Every time I tell someone that I am working in a Muslim country as a missionary they want to know what my platform is. Now, that said, understand that less than 5% of them are involved in a North African church. The average times that a missionary I have met in North Africa gives the gospel to someone maybe around one person a month. I would suggest to anyone going to a Muslim or Communist country that needs to have a platform to fight diligently to not lose focus of the main priority: The Great Commission.

25

May

My time has been obsessively thrown into language learning. I study the Bible in Arabic (usually I get through about 10 to 15 verses) in the morning from about 8-9 or 9:30. From there I head out on the streets talking to people, practicing a book that the Peace Corps uses to teach their volunteers the North African dialect of Arabic. The North African dialect and Classical Arabic share about 80% of the vocabulary but Classical Arabic uses a much more complicated system of grammar. I would put it about as close as Spanish is to Portuguese.

My favorite people on the street to learn from are a bunch of high school students who hang out and smoke hashish. They love teaching me. They usually gather around and fight for a chance to teach me something. They hang out on the steps of a French Catholic church, play their guitars, ride skateboards, and, yeah, smoke pot. In all the major cities there are a couple churches that were built more than fifty years ago when all of North Africa was under French control. Today they are allowed to exist to serve the international community only. North Africans are not allowed to enter more than one time. They are allowed in once to see the church and then never again. I don't know how they monitor that exactly but that's the law.

The students wear Iron Maiden, Metallica, and Def Leopard t-shirts. They read Marx, Lennon, and Che Guevarra. One of them I met even says he doesn't believe in God. He is a socialist. I have witnessed to two of them extensively in English: Mounir and Ishmael. I gave them both a New Testament. Mounir doesn't want to take the New Testament home in case his dad might find it and get mad. Pretty funny that he can smoke weed, have sex with his girlfriend, read books by atheists but not the Bible! No! That really shows the kind of power the Word of God has. Arabic Bibles and Christian material are against the law here. In any other language it's not illegal officially.

This week I memorized the story that Jesus told of the man who had two sons. One son promised his dad that he would go work in his vineyard and he didn't. The other son said that he wouldn't go, later repented, and then went to work. I have told this story to about ten North Africans and have asked them the same question Jesus asked, "Who did the will of the Father?" This exercise helps me with language immensely and also to understand their culture. Most have responded that the one who said he would go and then didn't is the one who did the will of the father. Of course this floored me so I asked why. The answer I got was that the son who refused to go when his father asked him shamed his father.

In Islam there is a principle that is much more important than right or wrong: Hashuma. Hashuma is what they say for shame. It is more acceptable to lie so as not be shameful than it would be to tell the truth. It is more acceptable to say you'll go and then just not show up than to shame yourself by refusing an invitation. I'd recommend this practice to anyone trying to learn a language or a culture.

After lunch Fatima, our baby sitter, comes while Jillian and I go for three hours of language school until 5 pm. The evenings are usually spent studying and/or talking with a lot of people who live and work right outside our door. Language learning is a 24-hour/7 day a week job. Arabic is listed as a level four language. Spanish is level one on the difficulty level. There are only four levels. So, we have a lot of work to do.

June

Mid-year Review

Praise the Lord for his mercies are new every morning. The job is more difficult than I had imagined. I was hoping to see someone become a follower of Christ by now and so far that hasn't happened. I can praise God for helping me communicate in Arabic more and more. I am able to preach short sermons, though riddled with mistakes, they are understandable.

July

From Aaron's Blog Ramblings from North Africa
www.projectnorthafrica.blogspot.com

Message of Hope Update
The Message of Hope Project is a project to mail the gospel in letter form from the US and other countries to Muslim homes in North Africa. Many of you have signed up and we are excited about what God is already doing through this project. Here are the facts:
-over 300 volunteers.
-120 individuals and 180 signed up through churches
-Goal of 30,000 mailouts before December

Pray for the 3,000 letters that will be going to homes in North Africa this month!

Goodbye to a few
I want to say goodbye and thank you to Heather from South Carolina. She was here with us for three weeks and was a great blessing. Last year I drove the 5 hours from Atlanta to her college to preach at their missionary prayer band. After the flop of a message that I delivered, we amazingly still had a good number of students express interest in coming with us to North Africa. Anyway, Heather was the ONLY student I met on the campus with a passion for reaching Muslims. She told me later on this trip that she had been touched by the tragedies in the Muslim world that she saw on the news. Just that semester she had surrendered her life to reach Muslims. She had never met a missionary doing it, though. No missionaries to Muslims amongst over twenty that came to her campus' missions conference, either. Just two days after asking God to send her someone, my wife and I came on to campus. Praise the Lord she signed up and came! I praise God for young people like her who would give her life to the most unpopular people on the face of this planet. Thanks, Heather! And thanks to her dad/pastor for encouraging her every step of the way.

Stephanie: God's Emailer

Stephanie is one of the interns working with Our Generation in North Africa. She has taken on the illustrious title of "Stephanie: God's Emailer". (Maybe you've heard of Bro. Andrew: God's Smuggler, well, she is much more famous.) She is industriously working around the clock to email North Africa for Jesus. She is collecting thousands of Emails of North Africans online. Next week, she will send her first "God's Email" in Arabic offering a free Jesus Film to over 1,000 people. From there she'll challenge their ideas of God, Salvation, and their souls. Pray for STEPHANIE: GOD'S Emailer!

We'll keep you up to date on the responses she receives.

Independence Day in North Africa

I have never spent my "Independence Day" in a country devoid of religious liberty until now. It was a mix of feelings to live in a place where it is illegal to witness for Christ yet look ahead to a day when liberty of religion will be granted. That is our dream. I told a believer friend of mine today that I dream of the day when everyone knows the Christians as they walk down the street without fear of imprisonment. First, however, we must dream of the uncomfortable day when Christians go to prison for their faith. The situation today is that there is no religious freedom nor are the churches here or around the world standing up against it. America was founded on this maxim: No man unwilling to fight for his freedom should have the privilege of enjoying it. Please pray today, for the courage of the church in the Muslim world.

I'd like to ask you to pray for Mohammed. He is a friend of mine who just received a Bible two days ago from a national believer. He was with me and that believer talking today. He has already read the first 10 chapters in Matthew! He is on his way and we are praying for his conversion. May the Lamb of God receive the recompense of his suffering.

Taxi drivers

My friend Jeff Bush once made taxi driver ministry popular in South America. Thanks, Jeff!

Anyway, over the last few days I have found myself in an unusual amount of taxis. Normally I walk everywhere I go because our office, my house, my language school, and the grocery store are all within a 10-minute walk. I have given out 3 New Testaments in Arabic in the last two days to taxi drivers. My heart was so burdened for them today. I asked our taxi driver if he has ever read the Injeel (New Testament). He says, "No, no! I am Muslim. I pray to Allah! Mohammed and Allah! Yep, Mohammed and Allah! I am a Muslim!"

He blurted it out like a record player. I could quickly tell that this guy was not one to be reasoned with, he just needs a direct blow to his memorized responses. So I went for the jugular, "Are you going to heaven when you die?" "Yes, yes! With God! Yes!" He said. "So, will I as well go to heaven?" I asked. "Yes. You too. Everyone who prays goes to heaven!" (Obviously he said that so as not to offend the American infidel sitting in his car knowing full well that I don't believe in his prophet." "Nope. You won't go to heaven. You'll go to hell." I countered. First time I've ever said that to a Muslim so bluntly on our first encounter. That was the first time he was speechless. I was able to explain to him his sin, mine, and the world's. Pray he'll read his New Testament along with the other two I was able to pass out yesterday.

Ever just get frustrated from "memorized responses" you get when trying to reason with a friend, son, daughter, boss? Make sure you know what the Bible says so you can give an answer for WHY you have hope in Christ!

Tabitha

The Lord put on my heart to preach about Tabitha this morning. You know, the lady in Acts 9 who when she died everybody cried and cried and sent Peter to raise her from the dead. Well, everybody cried because she was a giver. She wasn't a taker. She gave to the widows. She was all over the place giving till she had nothing left to give. Then, when she died, she left such a huge hole in the church that they just HAD to have Peter come and bring her back.

It made me think of a man named Brent who came and visited us in South America a couple years ago. He took time to get to know my wife and me. He was always looking for ways to serve. He even took care of our screaming 6-month-old son for hours in the airport. Brent is not a regular guy; he is Brent Armstrong, the pastor of a large church in Anderson, SC. He made an impact on me because he served me. Now in North Africa I wonder if I died today would I leave a hole in anyone's life? Or am I holding my life and finances so close that I can't help meet anyone's needs around me? I guess that is why I came to North Africa: I wanted to meet someone's unmet need for the gospel.

What hole would you leave if you left?

Can selfish be a personality?

This was written today by Micah, an American student who has grown a ton since he first arrived here 4 weeks ago:

"The Lord has used this trip to help me to overcome my fear of speaking to people. I realized that I was being selfish. I wouldn't talk to people about Jesus Christ because I didn't really care about them. This trip has opened my eyes about the lack of knowledge people have and the hopelessness their religion gives them concerning their eternity. They are so dedicated to a false god who will not help them. This convicted me because I have the truth and yet I will not share. Also that I worship the true God and I will not do what he says when he tells us to share the gospel to all nations and peoples. I have decided to be more dedicated to my Savior than they are to their god."

I thought that his thoughts are mirrored in many people's lives' including my own. Let's stop being selfish with the gospel and blaming it on our personality, location, or whatever else. Micah is going back to the US to immediately begin to prepare himself for full-time ministry at the Our Generation Training Center in Alpharetta, GA! Praise the Lord!

Music Evangelism

Here's a new idea for reaching Muslims: Music. I was in the office today when 3 of my friends came over. They are all punk rockers/hippies/anarchists/Muslims. (Seems like a lot of contradicting descriptions but that's what they are.) Anyway, they noticed my iPod and asked what I was listening to. Just so happens that I was listening to a CD a friend of mine recorded called All the Glory. They really liked the sound of the music and were interested when I told them it was Christian Music. You see, there is no such thing as Muslim music. Mohammed forbids any singing or instruments in reference to God though many Muslim scholars are divided on that one. I told them I'd give them a copy of the cd tomorrow along with the lyrics per their request. So, tomorrow we will discuss the words to this song:

"One man sinned, in the garden. A sin Jehovah could not condone. The bloodshed of animals could not forever, their sin atone. But the Son had compassion. He said Father, I'll be your lamb. Then once again, blood was shed. As the soldiers nailed his hands."

I've given New testaments to a couple of these guys. Please pray for them.

Good day in Church yesterday. The church we are going to had a new believer attending church for his first time. He was extremely excited. A couple friends of mine in another house church were able to lead Mohammed to Christ yesterday. Good day for Christ in North Africa. We need many, many more like it.

We were able to share the gospel for over an hour with Mouad the other night. We are praying that the words of the song I wrote out for him would be his song as well as many others who are now without the knowledge of the Savior and Redeemer of the world:

"Wonderful, merciful Savior. Precious redeemer and friend. Who would have thought that a lamb could rescue the souls of men.

Counselor, Comforter, Keeper, Spirit we long to embrace. You offer hope when our hearts are hopelessly lost our way. We've hopelessly lost the way.

You are the one that we praise. You are the one we adore. You give the healing and grace our hearts always hungered for. Our hearts always hungered for.

Almighty, infinite Father. Faithfully loving your own. Here in our

33

weakness you'll find us, falling before your throne. We're falling before your throne.

You are the one that we praise. You are the one we adore. You give the healing and grace our hearts always hungered for. Oh, our hearts always hungered for."

Friday: Full of dead men's bones

Friday always gets under my skin. I live in a very schizophrenic Muslim country. For six days a week a man may live selfish and ungodly. ON FRIDAY though, that same man may dress in a completely white robe from neck to the ground. Christ said that they are like whitened graves: Pure and beautiful on the outside but on the inside full of dead men's bones. Jesus got pretty angry at those types of people on a number of occasions. It ought to challenge all of us to humble ourselves and recognize our sinfulness.

Today we were walking from my office at 1:15 to eat at my house with two friends. We were met by a crowd of guys wearing their long robes at the exact same time. I commented to my friend, "Seems like we're going against the flow." We are praying for some to accept Christ and learn the joy and courage of walking against the flow. On the way we met up with a young man we have been witnessing to.

We are planning to invite 5 or 6 to this midweek service that we are holding along with a dinner that will follow. Will keep you updated!

To Accept or Not Accept

Mohammed, the guy I mentioned who had read ten chapters in the book of Matthew the other day, accepted Christ on Sunday with a friend of ours at another meeting we weren't present in. We praise our great God for that. He is studying English now with our interns in the evenings. He told me today, I am a Christian now like you! You are my friend...no...brother! Yeah, you are my brother!" I don't get emotional but we stopped on the street and hugged. Looking back it was kind of weird but, hey, call me weird.

While all the students studied English, we sat down with Mouad tonight for the second time and spent an hour and a half explaining Christ in the Bible. We spoke especially tonight about the prophecies

34

concerning Christ in the Old Testament. We read all of Isaiah 59. I hope that the Word will make some everlasting impact beyond anything I can say. On the way home we walked together and I asked him what he thought about what Isaiah said. (In case you don't know, Isaiah prophesied about one who would come to suffer and die for the sins of us all. Islam has no such idea and specifically rejects the idea of God sending someone to die.) I don't like to put myself out there like that but I really wanted to hear his thoughts after all our talk. He simply said, "I can't accept it."

My heart sunk to be honest. I felt like for two evenings we had poured our hearts out to him and opened the Bible and he was rejecting Christ. It hurt me for him because without faith in the Savior, there will be no forgiveness or hope for him. He said, "I am Muslim. Mohammed said that the Bible has been changed. I am not going to change." We'll keep praying for him and working with him as long as he comes around. Twenty years of indoctrination doesn't always disappear after a couple Bible studies.

When Paul would go into a city he would preach to the great multitudes and finally separate those who believed to further instruct them. Pray as we work on ways to preach to the multitude in these Muslim countries. The great majority won't accept Christ, but we are sure that many will. Islam in Arabia holds no power over the blood and conviction of our Savior!

God's Emailer Emails again!
Well, we just sent out our first "God's Emails" two hours ago. It was an email sent to almost 1,000 North African email addresses that one of the students, Stephanie, has collected over her last two months with us. In the email we told a story about Christ forgiving the woman caught in adultery then offered a free video about the life of Christ to anyone who would request it.

Bad news: a whopping 471 (Or 46.3%) bounced! Whoops.

Good news: In the first two hours after it has arrived in their inboxes 7 Muslims from all over the country have read the story and requested a video! We are looking forward to seeing what will happen over the next few days as people check their emails! From here we will mail a video with a list of questions that they can fill out and return to us.

Report from Interns in North Africa

A couple of the girls interning in North Africa had an opportunity to spend the night with the family of two of their friends, Sumaya and Miriam. Here is just a glimpse of what one of them wrote. More to come...

"It was unbelievable to think we were going to spend the night with a Muslim family that did not know about Jesus Christ. We were the first Christians that they had really met before. Before we went I prayed that God would open some type of door so we could tell them about the good news of Christ. The Lord heard and answered my prayer more then I would ever a think. They fed us a lot of food and they were so happy that we were there. Well their dad asked us to come and tape him praying. I did not under stand why because the people here really don't like that. As he was praying, I was praying that God would open doors and that they would see Christ in Paula and I. Well later that night Sumaya asked if we wanted to see her pray. Right before we all went to bed the girls asked if they could watch us pray. So we prayed together and asked God to open there eyes and just thanked him for what he was doing and what he was going to do. When we finished we looked up and Sumaya was crying."

"There is not god but Allah"...or is there?

There aren't very many agnostics in Muslim North Africa. The first words that enter their ears at birth are, "There is no god but Allah and Mohammed is his prophet." The first verse they are taught from the Koran as a child is, "God is one and God is great. He can not have children nor can he give birth." I found one however in my friend Redouan. Redouan's dad split when he was young so he and his older brother have been the men of the house. He works a job where he makes around $200/month as a security guard. He was one of my first language helpers.

As I got to know him a few months ago he told me how money is what is important to him, not God. With all the pain in the world, he couldn't understand how an all-powerful God could actually exist. A few months ago he came to a Bible study we were having at a friend's house. He didn't understand much of it because it was in Spanish (we didn't know much Arabic back then). So I hadn't seen him in more than 2 months as of yesterday. I stopped by his work just to say hi. As we talked he asked me, "When are you guys having another meeting? I'd like to go." So we planned for him to come to the next one. As we were saying goodbye he told me, "When I talk to God he never answers me. But when you talk to God it's as if you know he is listening." There are many searching like Redouan. The job now is to find them and give them the truth.

Also, the two girls who came to our Bible study last night argued with us afterwards the whole time. Today they asked if we were having another one tonight because they'd like to come. We aren't, but will be in a few days so we invited them to that. Pray for women in Muslim countries to come to know Christ. The male believers in Christ outnumber the females by 4 to 1. That is mostly due to the attitude toward women in Islam. They don't dare think for themselves or investigate the truth. They belong to their fathers until the day they are "sold" to their husbands. Pray for these ladies.

Youth Camp

Well, ok, not really. A Muslim friend of mine, named Redouan (not the same one I just mentioned) who lives in the boonies (far away) always wants us to go camping and fishing there with him. We have been once before and had a great, relaxing time so I told him we would go yesterday and today. It would be a great opportunity for me to witness to him as well. I gave him a "More than a Carpenter" book a while back. So we headed out yesterday and a new believer, Mohammed, came with us. With all the ladies in the house around midnight, us fellas (2 Muslims, 2 Americans, and 1 new Christian) sat around a communal meal cooked on a campfire by the side of a large lake. I prayed for the food and included a prayer for them. Of course that opened up conversation.

Something I wasn't expecting though is that Mohammed, who has been saved less than two weeks, began questioning Islam right away. They didn't know he was a believer in Christ but after less than ten minutes they asked him the question he couldn't wiggle out of, "You believe in Jesus AND Mohammed, right?" I was nervous for him as I saw his mind racing for the right answer and his faith led him to say, "I believe in Jesus." Then it started. Almost two hours of arguing. I was out of it as the foreigner who didn't understand half of what they were rattling off to each other. I only butted in a few times to make sure that the new believer got his fair chance to be heard. He held his ground and was very bold. I was very proud of him.

Around 2 am we all crammed into the two-man tent and awkwardly went to sleep. More awkward than our close proximity was the no-solutions conversation/fight we had just had. In the morning Mohammed, Micah, and I got up at 6 am and went to read our Bible while my Muslim friends slept to around 9. We had an awesome time in the scripture. Mohammed was very encouraged to know that resistance to his new beliefs is more normal that PB and J (except here maybe Hummus and bread). We read many verses and finally landed on Romans 12:1, "Therefore my beloved brethren, I beseech you by the mercies of Christ that you present your bodies a living sacrifice, Holy, acceptable unto God which is your reasonable service." We memorized it together and settled on a nickname, we would call my friend Mohammed the rest of the day: living sacrifice. He kind of liked it. Especially he liked to tell our Muslim friends his new nickname after they woke up.

Redouan didn't mind me witnessing to him but as soon as he found out that Muslims are accepting Christ our relationship has changed. He warned me about the police and the anti-conversion law.

So that was kind of like a two day Youth Camp for us. Please pray for Mohammed to grow stronger as he will undoubtedly face MUCH more opposition from this family and friends. Ramadan is soon approaching so there will be no hiding then.

Preaching For six months here we haven't preached as we have been learning the language. Like Jeremiah, it is a fire in our bones that must get out. This week was our first Sunday to invite our lost friends to come. We had four Muslims come and a total of 13 in attendance. I preached for around 30 minutes on "Ye must be born again" from John 3. I did it twice, actually, since one fella couldn't come at the time we originally planned. These being our first services in a Muslim country where unbelievers are present we had no idea how to do everything. Should we sing? To sing to God is forbidden in Islam. Should we sing about Jesus, the Son of God? That might offend them right away and they may not hear the message. Not knowing what to do we decided to sing a couple songs about how great God is and then have the preaching in the first service. Without exception all of the Muslims started quickly writing down the words to our songs and singing along with us.

After the meeting, Redouan the Agnostic asked me "How do I get this new life? What if I sin again in my new spirit?" and a many other questions. After spending an hour reading Isaiah 53 and half of the book of John we came back to my house to watch a video about the life of Christ. That's what he is doing right now as I am writing this. Pray for him.

Another Testimony

The students just left North Africa this morning. They are going to be working hard to recruit for next years trip. Paula wrote this after she spent a night in the home of two Muslim young ladies that she and Stephanie had befriended:

"This night was awesome!!! I think that it was the best night that I spent in North Africa. The girls and their family were awesome!!!! We were the first Americans that had been to their house. They wanted us to film everything in their house, even when their father prayed. Steph and I were praying too. It was crazy to have two Christians and one Muslim in the room praying. I am so thankful that I know God hears our prayers!! Then we filmed Sumaya pray. Later they wanted to see us pray. We prayed and Sumaya started crying. I think that she couldn't believe what it was like for us. Then she asked many questions and I was able to share with her how Jesus died for my sins and the sins of the whole world. I told her that I know for sure where I will spend eternity. She said there is no way to know. She came back with many answers from Islam, but I could tell that she was very interested in Christianity and would want it, but they are drilled in Islam and don't think it could be possible for them. Steph gave her a Bible and she took it. It was an awesome experience. That night God did a big work in my heart and helped me surrender to missions. I am so glad I got to have this experience. Since that night the girls have come to two church services where they have been able to hear the plan of salvation without a language barrier.

This trip gave me lots of amazing experiences. We were able to meet with many North Africans, teach English, spend two nights in North African homes, see people come to church services, share the Gospel, get hands on training for ministry, and many other amazing experiences. This trip definitely gave me a greater burden for lost people not just in North Africa but around the world as well."

New Men Needed

I am finishing reading the 250 page Biography on Samuel Zwemmer. Wow! I feel like a bum. He spent 60 years of his life selflessly serving Christ amongst Muslims. He wrote his first book "Arabia" at 33. Not TOO impressive, right. Except it was 450 hand written pages. He went on to write over 50 books as well as being the editor of "The Moslem World" quarterly for 25 years. He traveled from America to South Africa to China surveying the Muslims of the world. He lost two daughters on the Arabian Peninsula. He preached in English, Dutch, and Arabic.

Anyway, amazing guy. Toward the end of his missionary ministry while in his 60's he was addressing a group of missionaries in China. There was a lot of talk, like there always is amongst the young and ambitious, about all the mistakes in methods the "old missionaries" had developed. Now, we should always be questioning the systems to make sure we are getting the desired result BUT Dr. Zwemmer expressed what could not be truer almost 100 years later:

"In rethinking missions, it is not the want of new methods that should give us the most anxiety. The modern missionary needs to listen more to the 'voice behind thee saying, this is the way walk ye in it. We none of us like to listen to back seat driving but it was what we needed most. We should listen in these days to the voice of those days, to the voice of those in the back seat, the early missionary pioneers, the apostles who succeeded where we have failed. An analysis of the lives of these great men, who first opened various countries to the Gospel, revealed that they possessed several qualities sometimes absent from the modern missionary. Notable amongst these qualities are: Vision, knowledge of the language and people, persistence, passion for souls and ability to endure loneliness. It is a new man rather than a new method that is most wanting."

Ouch. That stings. But true.

Student Intern Testimony

Micah just left us on Monday. I can honestly say I have never seen a person change as much as he did in a six-week period. His fellow students commented that he doesn't seem like the same person. Check out what God did in his life:

"I came to North Africa as an intern for the wrong reasons. I did not expect anything to happen in my heart while I was over here. However God has worked through the trip to open my eyes to what he would have me to do with my life.

Before coming to North Africa I could have been described as a shy person. I have learned however that the only way to be a real winner in life is to allow God to work through our weaknesses. As an intern God has helped me to overcome my fear of speaking in front of people. I was able to teach an English class and to preach twice. I witnessed to my first person here, a Muslim named Hicham. The same day that I met Hicham he took off work to come and speak to me more. We spoke for three hours the first night and I was able to witness to him. Since then we have spoken a couple more times and I have been able to witness to him some more. He started to read the Bible that I gave him and he is almost through the New Testament.

I was able to see much of the country and I saw the darkness of Islam more than ever before. I was able to go to attend a North African church and see the people here worship God even though they could be persecuted for it. This convicted me about my lack being an open witness of the gospel in one of the freest countries of the world. The Lord used the missionaries to show me what it is like to be a missionary. The Lord has used this trip to help me to see what it is like to teach people. That it is a blessing if it is done right and for the right reasons. If we do not tell share the gospel when we have the opportunity we are not obeying Christ's commission. I now have a very strong desire to impact the world with my life because I was able to have a small impact in a few people's lives as a PNA Intern. "

Pray for 22 Koreans in Afghanistan

We want to beg your prayers for 22 South Koreans being held hostage by the Taliban in Afghanistan. The new government is under extreme pressure now as they try to not negotiate with terrorists. The leader of the group was already shot to death. Militant Islam is Islam the way Mohammed meant it to be. We must all get involved in the very real spiritual battle of sharing the love of Christ with the 1.3 billion Muslims in this world. God wills it. We must surrender to his will and obey.

Afghanistan is #10 in the World Watch List for persecution of Christians. That is down from its #3 pre-war ranking.

Sunday Report

Couple "firsts" to be excited about today:
1. Preached today in Arabic on the Lamb of God as described by the Old Testament prophets. First time that I preached from multiple passages (about 8) and first time I preached 40 minutes. (Not sure if that is a good thing or not). It took me about 6 hours of study to make it happen. We had a small crowd of only 8 people so it was more of a group Bible study than a straight monologue.

2. A few weeks ago I reported on a mass email we sent out to 1,000 North Africans thanks to Stephanie, an intern here with us from South Carolina. A number of people responded asking for a Jesus Film. One of those was from our city, a man named Husain. Today a believer named Said who is growing leaps and bounds, and myself went to visit Husain in order to deliver his Jesus Film personally. Now, if you know anything about missions in a Muslim country that is a big move for him as a new believer. Neither he nor I had ever made a "cold call" like this before. Everyone has heard the stories of under-cover police or Muslim extremists.

As we looked for the man's address we walked through the Suq (Arab Market) as if God was guiding us since we had no idea where this street was. Within a short time my friend Said looked up and recognized the name of the street. We found that the address was a second floor Internet cafe. I waited downstairs (like the lazy American usually does) while Said went upstairs and inquired of the man by name. When Said came downstairs he was laughing. "He has a big Muslim beard and dress" he laughed. (My brother calls it a "Man Dress".) Now a beard here almost always signifies a Muslim radical. Said didn't run though so neither did I. The man who turned out to be the owner of Internet cafe came down and stood nervously as my Said introduced us to each other. We thanked him for his request. He kept repeating, "I never expected anybody to come visit me." He told us what he really wants is a Bible to learn about what the other prophets said. "Why do you want it since the Koran holds all you need to know?" asked Said. "I want to learn. The Koran doesn't tell me much about the other prophets." So we took his phone number and left him the Jesus Film, all on the street outside his business.

As we walked away we prayed for him. Said told me that it was the first time that he had witnessed without being scared at all. He said something that I love and think ought to be preached all over the Muslim world: "I was thinking, if I accepted Christ, he saved me, and now I serve the true, all-powerful God, what do I have to fear of these Muslims. There is no fear in faith."

3. I saw the king yesterday. My first king to see in person. This country is the last kingdom in Africa and thus, the last country with a king. My friend Said and I were on our way to meet Husain in the service of the King of Kings when we noticed all the main street was shut down to traffic and a crowd was gathering on the sides of the street. What seemed like hundreds of cops started blowing their whistles rapidly. A stream of black Mercedes followed surrounded by police motorcycles. Then came the king. Surrounded by about twenty motorcycles his black Mercedes was specially fitted with a sunroof that allowed him to stand halfway out of the car and wave to all the peasants. His car was also surrounded on all four corners by 4 other black Mercedes with the two back doors open and body guards standing with suits flying in the wind. Really quite the spectacle. He is not my king but I was very impressed.

I can't imagine the feelings that will come over me someday when we all stand in the presence of Our King and worship him. When I am able to touch his hands and feet and lay any crowns I will have obtained at his feet. It's going to be awesome!

August

First Responder from the Message of Hope
Just got an email last week from Othman here in our city. We translated the following into English:

"Peace upon you Christian brothers and sisters. I received your letter but I want to know more about Christianity. So I hope that you send me a New Testament as soon as possible.

I hope to receive it as a book, not as on a CD because I don't have a computer. Thank you very much."

We will be in touch with him and even visiting him this week, Lord willing. Please pray for that meeting. God is not willing that Othman would perish but that he would come to repentance!

What don't I like about Islam? Hmmm?
On my way home from the office the other day with my friend and coworker, Said. We stopped for a haircut. The barber, always the zealous Muslim asked me if I am a Muslim yet. They always say that. Gets under my skin. "Are you a Muslim **yet**?" How am I supposed to answer? Anyway, when I say no he tells me I ought to read the Koran. When I say, "Yeah, I have read it and now I really don't want to be a Muslim." He looks surprised and asks me an impossible question, "What don't you like about Islam?"

Well, I take a deep breath and say,

-It's prophet
-It's book
-It's morals
-It's revisionist history
-It's intolerance
-It's hatred
-It's ...

I could go on.

No, I didn't say that. I simply told him, "You don't really want to know and walked out of the shop." He begged me to tell him but seeing as he has never read about my Savior, I know he wouldn't understand. He implored my friend Said to convince me of Islam. Said of course said, "Well, you convince me first then I'll convince him." That made him furious.

See, didn't think he really wanted to know what I don't like about Islam.

I have to answer questions here most have never even pondered answers for. The people are prepared against the Christian message of Christ with hard questions and often harder hearts. I am often the subject of proselytization BUT how can we say that these people are hard hearted if they have never heard a Christian hymn? Never read the life of Jesus? Never met a true believer in Christ? Never heard a Christian talk to his Father? Never held God's message in their language?

We realize by choosing Arab Muslims we may have chosen the most resistant field on this planet to the gospel but I have to ask myself, "Have they even yet began to resist?

We wouldn't have a future
Project North Africa has as it's first goal: "The mobilization of WELL-TRAINED laborers to the Muslims of North Africa." Latin America, a long time mission field, is now a huge pool of new workers.

Tyler and his wife Gretchen surrendered to reach the Muslims in North Africa a couple years ago. God used him to co-found Project North Africa and work specifically to recruit, train, and mobilize Latinos and Americans for the work. He is living in Latin America doing that right now. This summer Tyler brought a group of 9 students to North Africa. Two surrendered to missions and are on their way for training right now. Tyler flew from South America to the U.S. to train the students, then from the U.S. to North Africa to be with us. In all he spent thousands of dollars and much time and effort in order to raise up these laborers. We desperately need laborers to come and be a part of this harvest going on in the Muslim world. We may be on the front lines talking with the Muslims face to face each day but without the recruiting and training going on now, we wouldn't have a future. Soon he'll be over here with us and will be missed there.

"Grant thy servants BOLDNESS"

Act 4:29 "And now, Lord, behold their threatenings: and grant unto thy servants, that with all boldness they may speak thy word"

A lot of debate goes on about how to reach the "closed countries" of this world. Those are mostly in the 10-40 Window and almost without exception Muslim or Communist. Arguments are made for strategies of mass evangelism: "If we could only get Satellite TV programs going." Arguments are made for business as mission: "What we need are Christians to live amongst the people in business." Discipleship, church planting, yada, yada, yada. Of which, I am in favor of all of them.

However, the ONE thing that we must have and must ask God for is **BOLDNESS**. Without boldness the Muslim world will never see our faith in Christ because fear is the opposite of faith. Over the next few days I will be giving stories of BOLDNESS here in North Africa and in the history of the church:

I told you a few days ago how Said and I visited a man named Husain at his business. A few days ago, an email came to us as a response to the <u>Message of Hope Project</u> that is mailing thousands of letters a month to Muslims here in our country. Othman asked for an Old Testament so he could read about the prophets. Said and I set out today for our second visit. We had looked for Othman's address before in vain. Today Said decided after 2.5 hours of fruitless searching (streets are not marked well here) to pray and ask God to show him the address. After he finished praying he looked up to see a man that he knew in the distance. He followed after him for about a block when he looked up and saw, you guessed it, the name of the street we had been looking for. He called me right away and together we went to knock on Othman's door.

Before knocking on the door I asked Said what name he wanted to be called by. Many national believers in the Muslim world don't

46

want to be known by their real name for fear of persecution. Said replied, "By my name, of course. I'm not going to lie." Ooops. I felt like a stooge.

After summoning a confused Othman down to the alley where he lived we told him the reason for our visit. He was a 26 year old, slightly chubby young man dressed in a djellaba. He greeted us with a smile and great surprise. Said asked him why he wanted the Bible and he responded, as did Husain: "To read about the lives of the prophets that are mentioned in the Koran (Adam, Noah, Abraham, David, Solomon, etc). Directly after his response he asked Said,
O: "Are you Muslim?"
S: "What do you suppose?"
O: "Well are you?"
S: "No..I am a Christian."
O: Stunned silence. "But...you're name is Muslim"
S:"Yes. I was a Muslim."
O: "Are you from here?"
S: "Yes."
O: "Really?"
S: "Really."
O: "No, really?"
S: "Yes, really."
O: "These foreigners have lied to you and fooled you."
S: "No. I became a Christian before I talked to any of these foreigners."
O: "What's your problem with Muslims?"
S: "I don't have a problem with Muslims. They are all my brothers. My problem is with Mohammed and the Koran."
O: "Oh, well, maybe I'll take you to an Imam and he can convince you."

And that is how the conversation went on Othman's front door step. Othman was stunned to meet a Muslim turned Christian. Said was able to share with him some truths from the Old Testament that point to Christ. We exchanged phone numbers and decided to meet again. The most encouraging thing he said was, "Since you know so much about Islam and Christianity, I think I could learn a lot from you."

Said is learning directly from God's Word what it means to have

BOLDNESS not from watching the Christian trends around him. That one character trait is the one thing that made Paul the greatest preacher the world has ever known. He was unequivocally BOLD. Our job is to BOLDLY witness for Christ. God's job is to guide us, protect us, and in the end, use us to lift his name high for the world to see.

Monday Bible Study
What must death be like for the Mohammedan? How do they deal with it when a family member dies?

Well, there is a lot of wailing on the part of the woman. A lot of rituals that must be performed and a lot of prayers go up for the deceased ones that Allah will grant forgiveness. Today I met Mustapha at our Bible study. There were 6 there in total. Mustapha's young brother tragically drowned last week. I tried to talk to Mustapha about it but he has a very reserved, no-emotion type personality it seems that he has been perfecting for the last 30 years. His brother was only 16 when he went with some friends and was pulled under by a current. They found his body just a couple days ago.

Mustapha enjoyed our songs and asked for a copy of them. He went home with a New Testament after hearing an absolute bomb of a message from me. God humbled my confidence in Arabic today, that is for sure. Ever have a day when you feel that every attempt at expressing yourself is futile? Now imagine that feeling in Arabic, Chinese, Xhosa or some other language your missionaries are learning! Even my ever-consistent friend and colaborer Said said to me after my "message", "Man, you can't say anything today!" Thanks God, for the lesson! I'll work harder.

How they get by
Learning a language is also an experience in learning a culture. How people make "flus" (money) to survive is a vital part of that.

So I always see this guy, Hassan, sitting at the corner close to my house at a coffee shop. He and others tell me that he is a "car salesman". I always say hi to him and shake his hand as I pass by every day because I feel this bond. He is from the same town in the south that Khalid is from at Vision Baptist Church. Khalid was one of the first ex-Muslims I ever met. I met him last January at Atlanta Bread Company. He joined the church we were working in and we've been great friends ever since. So, back to Hassan. I sat with him today during a brief lull in activity after language school. We began to talk and I found this out about his job:

-He buys and sells cars. That coffee shop is his office. He parks his car (literally, he has an 8 year old Mercedes for sale now) in front of the coffee shop and waits for inquirers. He owns one car at a time and will wait to sell it. When it sells he'll buy another and wait some more. Some months he sells his car. Some months he doesn't. He has been sitting at that coffee shop just like that for more than ten years! That's a lot of sitting and a lot of tea. Crazy life. Can you imagine sitting all day everyday staring at the same car just waiting to sell it! Luckily he is single so he can live on tea alone.

-Karim is the guy who sits with Hasan every day. He is into another kind of buying/selling. He sells individual cigs. He'll buy a few packs for $2 each and then with their individual sale make 50 cents per pack. He sells maybe 5 packs per day. Add it up folks: $2.50/day. I don't know how he eats because the tea where he sits is almost 50 cents. Don't really get that one but don't want to dig too much.

-My doorman, Mohammed, makes, on paper, probably $150. He gets tips so he may make up to $200 or more. Not sure exactly. So I noticed that he smokes constantly. I asked him how much and he tells me a pack per day. We figured that up together to cost him around $50/month. Not too smart. He promises to quit but we'll see.

-Young man who accepted Christ just a few weeks ago named Mohammed told me that his family's crop in the mountains is hashish (wacky weed, Mary Jane, whatever). Turns out that a crop of that will yield 14 times the profit of a legal crop. Not sure what that profit is, though.

So that's a brief synopsis of how people get by in North Africa.

Wednesday Night Mind Dump

Too many things on my mind to expound on one so I'll just blab:

-Spanish service went well tonight. Did it half in Spanish actually. Had 4 nationals, 5 native Spanish speakers, and my wife and I gathered around the Word. It was really a good time. One Muslim there.

-Excited about upcoming trip. Taking a trip on a train to multiple destinations next week. We will be visiting homes of those who have asked for Bible all along the way. We've never done this before so we're excited. Our dream is to see people accepting Christ all over the country. We'll make it all the way to the border of the neighboring country, Lord willing. I will update you on that one.

-Had a police walk through today at our office… unannounced. I was fortunately sitting surrounded by three computers and a printer going full blast printing language material as four people were in the other room having class. Everything checks out! (Except for two Arabic Bibles my friend Said left sitting on the desk. Those are illegal in this country.) He snooped around quite a bit but didn't see anything he shouldn't have. Praise our God.

-Had a GREAT time rolling around on the ground with the kids after arriving home at 9:30. I've been playing with them until now (11:15). It's a real de-stresser for a pretty stressful day.

-Translating our own language school material every morning. Not easy work. Fairly frustrating since this dialect of Arabic is spoken is not written.

-I've got an awesome wife. She is juggling a visit from family, 2 kids, 3 hours of language school (in her 3rd language), her husband, and ministry.

Patience is a virtue

At least that's what every kid hears. (Seems obvious doesn't it? Why is THAT a saying? There are hundreds of virtues. Maybe if it were, "Patience is THE virtue" it would be quotable. Anyway.) I was on a two-day trip to a town about 3 hours from here this weekend and I can tell culture shock set in. I don't like to admit culture shock but I would have to this time. I'd like to blame it on my mother in law who was traveling with us but...

Blowup #1:

So I sit down at a restaurant to have tea with my kids while my wife and mother-in-law are out shopping. A national introduced himself and told me that his wife is American. Interesting. So we talked about it and in the conversation it came up that I am a Christian and I said it in a fairly convincing way. Something like, "100%" or something. So a young man who was listening sits down across from me at the table. I welcome him and without responding with politeness he starts quoting the Koran about how there is one God and Mohammed is his prophet. Ticked me off. I just sat down and was having a friendly conversation with his friend and didn't ask him to sit at my table or start quoting the Koran. I held my cool though and told him if he like to sit and talk he could stay but if he wants to quote the Koran for me I've already read it.

I asked him if he has read the Bible and he says, "Yes". Of course I know he hasn't because NONE of them have. He says, "Its all in the Koran." Maybe it's the way he said it (or maybe my mother-in-law) but I just couldn't take it. I told him all I really think about his prophet and the book he wrote. Then I called him a liar (for insisting that he has read the Bible when he hasn't) and ignorant (for not being willing to). I told him he was not welcome to sit at my table and be a lying ignoramus. So...he left. It was a fairly audible conversation. (I'd like to lie and tell you only the nice parts but that's really what happened.)

Blow up #2

Feeling bad for that one I entered into a shop the next day in the same town and looked at the TV. They were selling a special edition Koran. I asked a few questions about it. The young man there asked, "Are you a Muslim." To which I gave the same reply, "No, Christian." To which he conjectured, "Not yet a Muslim then." I insisted, "I am a Christian, 100%." He said, "Maybe 99%?" I responded, "No, 100." Then another young man in the store said, "Not good". In English. After I asked him to clarify what he said I told him that on the same token I don't think it's good that he's a

51

Muslim. The storeowner soon arrived to whom I explained that if he doesn't teach those working at his store a little common sense and courtesy that I would not be back. He apologized for them though they never did. Something about it just ticked me off. Another opportunity to share the love and patience that only Christ gives was lost.

Why do I tell you all that? I know, I am a bad Christian. But when you hear ignorant stuff like that every day for seven months now you get a little weary (or I do). Patience is no longer patience when it runs out. Just like obedience isn't obedience if you stop obeying. So, I lost patience. Now, if I let that fester in my heart and have an attitude like that ongoing my fruit here amongst Muslims will be limited. Why? Patience is a farmers #1 attribute: "But that on the good ground are they, which in an honest and good heart, having heard the word, keep it, and bring forth fruit with patience." (Luke 8:15)

I had to go to church that same day where I worshipped Christ with more than 20 ex-Muslims who were just as ignorant and stubborn as those others were before Christ changed them. I, in fact, am often ignorant and stubborn and Christ's blood forgives even me. If I were born in Muslim Arabia my passion for my own ignorant beliefs would no doubt exceed all those whom I have met here so far. I, Christ's servant, have no reason or room for impatience.

Trip Report

Wow. I don't know where to start. I left on Monday for Project North Africa's first "Follow-up Trip". My goal was to make it to the far east city of the country stopping along the way to visit those who have contacted us through our website and Email Evangelism that the Intern Students worked on while there were here.

Now it is Wednesday and I am geographically over half way to our goal. So much has happened as I sit in this Internet cafe waiting on our next contact to meet with me. I am really bad at recounting these things. I tend to do it by bullet point. I'll do my best:

Day 1: Monday

Left around 4 pm in taxi. My first contact was Mohammed. He

accepted Christ over a month ago now and now is back on his family's farm about 3 hours from my city. After two crowed taxis rides where everyone wanted to talk about why I should be a Muslim, I arrived in the base city, half an hour from Mohammed's family's farm. It was 7 pm by then and I learned an important lesson: travel early. In the evening, there are few passengers, thus, not enough to fill up a taxi to take me to the next city. They wanted $24 for a 30-minute ride since I would be the only passenger! Around 8 pm ten others arrived wanting to go about twenty minutes past my destination on the same road. Problem: They already know the foreigner is willing to pay the money if he has to in order to get there. So, I ended up paying $18 and they all paid $4 a piece! Just gotta laugh and pay up sometimes.

So I arrived at Mohammed's house around 9 pm. On a lonely mountain road at night he was waiting for me at the only building standing by the side of the road: a coffee stand. After hugs and an awesome apple/milk juice we headed by foot over a couple mountain ridges to his house. He is the only believer in about a half hour radius. "I missed you! I feel all alone here!" He exclaimed. That became the theme of what I wanted to teach him while I was there with him, "You are NEVER alone when Christ is with you." Now, to put that into practice!

On the way to his house we walked through a field of wacky weed and finally arrived where his mom and little brother were waiting for us with a freshly killed and cooked chicken! Delicious. Though he has had the courage to tell a few strangers that he is a Christian he has not yet told his family. He is afraid he'll be out on the street. Pray for him to have courage to stand for Christ. He is his family's only hope. After dinner we went through the dark, on paths that he knew so well that he didn't need a light, over the next hill to where his dad was working. His dad was working all through the night when the police would be sleeping with four workers to produce about $3000 worth of marijuana in one night. I've never seen anything like it. They all acted like it was pretty normal, though, as we got to know each other lying on the steep hill where they couldn't be seen. Later that night we slept on his roof (it is flat) under millions of the brightest stars I have ever seen.

The next morning, Tuesday, we were up early to have breakfast with

53

his dad who hadn't slept yet. From there we went to pick grapes for his little brother to sell on the side of the road for $1.20/kilo. We took our New Testament with us and stopped by the river to do our morning devos. I taught him how to do those the last time we were together but like most new babes, he needs more coaching than that. Last time we read John 1. He had managed John 2 by himself but from there he would just do the whole "open and read" thing. So we set in the shade of a cliff next to the river and had a great time praying and reading John 3. He understood baptism for the first time and was encouraged about what it means to be born again. He knows he is. Praise God alone.

The rest of the morning was spent talking about all that we had read in the Word as we worked in his dad's vineyard until my departure at 2 pm for my next city and next contact.

Day 2 On day two of my trip I left my friend Mohammed. His dad and I waited about 30 minutes by the side of the road until a taxi came by with a couple empty spots. The taxis are Mercedes imported from Europe after they were done using them. They are all about as old as I am. We arrived in the next town about 30 minutes later where Mohammed's dad was going to "the Suq" and I was moving on to the next city to meet my next contact. I gathered a couple guys going to the same place, got a better deal this time than I did last time. I was the only foreigner and we were off on the two-hour trip.

As I sat in the back with three other guys I noticed a Police check point about halfway to our destination. I have only been stopped once at these checkpoints. They usually wave us on. This one stopped us. I don't know why but I got nervous. Maybe it was the stash of Bibles and books I had in my backpack in the trunk. The officer smiled at my blue passport and tried to speak to me in English for a few minutes, concluded with "Marhababik" (welcome), and we were on our way. The rest of the passengers laughed at me the rest of the way for acting as if I only speak English. I find that is the best way to deal with Police though.

Anyway, at my destination I gave my contact Ali a call. Now we had received an email from Ali over a year ago. He said that is 19 and a believer in Christ. The webmaster from Lebanon had been in touch with him via Internet but we had never met him. I met him at a park adjacent to a rotisserie chicken restaurant. As I sat eating dinner he told me his story:

-When he was 19 years old he had a dream. Somebody appeared and handed him a book that said, "Injeel" (New Testament). He immediately started looking for an Injeel on the Internet and found a phone number he could call. When he talked to this person on the other end she told him that God was trying to show himself to Ali. He immediately accepted Christ as his Savior. He began to receive Bibles and other literature through the mail. Along with our website, www.arabicbible.com, he was also receiving literature from Walk Through the Bible with J. Vernon McGee in English and a few other places. He has already read the whole New Testament and parts of the Old.

His parents soon began to realize the pile of letters and books he was receiving. His dad is a serious Muslim and was not at all happy. He took all his books and put them in water and then burned them. When Ali persisted in following Christ he refused to give him any money to go back to the University he was attending in his second year. Now Ali is 21. He has met many Christians online but has only met one believer face to face. When he was going through these hard times with his family the believer he met wouldn't help him. According to his story, he would call this believer and he would always say that he was too busy. Ali told me that this hurt him since he really needed a friend and brother to stand by him and encourage him, as you can imagine.

Ali's brothers and sisters were sympathetic toward him. They always tried to make his dad quit treating him badly. Whenever a letter or book would come, his sister Talia, who is still a Muslim, would hide it from their dad and give it to him. Now Ali is out of his parent's house and living with that sister so he has more freedom. He has witnessed to many of his friends about Christ and has given them New Testaments that he would receive in the mail.

They craziest thing about Ali you haven't heard yet though, is that he speaks English AND Chinese! So, I know his English is fluent but I had no way of testing his Chinese against mine (non-existent). He invited me to spend the night at his house. Upon arrival we "skyped" my friend in China (www.gospelinchina.wordpress.com). They held about a five-minute conversation in Chinese. Ali also chats with Chinese almost everyday on line using Chinese characters! Stinking genius. Learned it all from a couple Chinese friends he has in the country.

Please pray for Ali:

-He needs a job. His dad wouldn't let him finish University as his punishment for following Christ so he has yet to find a job.
-He wants to get baptized. I asked him all the questions and he knew the Biblical answer.
-He needs encouragement. I told him that if at any moment he needed encouragement or found himself in a jam that I would be on the next train, plane, or automobile to be there for him. "That means a lot to me", he responded. What he really needs is to be a part of a living New Testament church. We will work on that.

We got up early on day three at his house and did our devotions together. He had done his assignment that I had given him the night before of reading through the book of Philippians. What did he get out of it? "Paul lost everything just to win Christ...and he was happy about it!" I left Ali at the train station and headed to my next destination. Thank God for www.alnour.com and www.arabicbible.com that has made such an impact on his life. If you or someone you know has mad techy skills we need a webmaster for this ministry that is touching thousands of lives of Muslims and ex-Muslims alike.

So what did I learn from Ali:

-I have no excuses to feel discouraged. I have many brothers in Christ who would be there for me at a moments notice if I need them.
-There are people like him all over the Muslim world who need a church. I just talked to a guy on the phone in his same situation south of here: new Christian, no church.

Anybody willing to move and start one?

<u>Day 3</u> So on Wednesday morning Ali and I woke up and talked about what he had read in the book of Philippians. It was the first time he had ever read the Bible together in person with a fellow believer. I keep thinking about how amazing that is that he could grow like he has alone with just the Word of God and the study materials he was receiving in the mail. At breakfast with his family I prayed that God would bless the food and their home in the name of Christ. I plan on taking my wife and kids next time we visit so she can get to know his sister and begin to witness. Pray for the rest of his family. Ali lives in a city of over 1.5 million people known as the center of Islamic teaching for the country. This city desperately needs a preacher.

The 11 am train found me on it on my way to the next city. I sat across from a guy who kept mumbling quite inaudibly classical Arabic to me and ending his sentences with an inquisitive look (looked more like a twitch) that was intended to signify that he was asking me a question. After about ten annoying minutes of that he realized I didn't understand and switched to the local dialect which I quickly grasped. After exchanging names and professions his first question was: "Do you teach people about Jesus at your business?" Maybe I have "Missionary" written on my forehead or something. I immediately got a little nervous. Thoughts ran through my mind, "Is he the police? Is he following me? Oh wait, I sat next to him, not him to me. Is he going to start blowing a whistle when I tell him I do?" Anyway, I responded, "That's not the purpose of my business but I do teach people about Christ anytime I can." I followed by saying that it's against the law to tell people about Christ to which he reacted strongly. "No it's not! Against the law?! No! You can say anything you want!" Sure, sure.

Many people here like this man or either lying through their teeth or they are deceiving themselves into imagining that there is freedom of speech and religion. This man is not alone. Most people will attest that their country is free and they are free to believe what they want. Even though the law clearly states prison time as the consequence of "shaking the faith of a Muslim" or "rejecting Islam and its prophet." The rest of the train ride was fairly quiet. The terrain on the way is dry mountainous desert reminding me of the hearts of the people inside the train.

By the time I arrived at the next city I was 9 hours from my original starting point. Population 250,000. I met contact #3, Karim, at a coffee house around 4 pm. He kissed my cheeks 4 times, sat next to me and whispered, "There are spy's here. Come with me." All I knew about Karim was that he had been in touch with a national pastor for about a month and wanted a whole Bible as he was already in possession of a New Testament. As we walked and talked I learned that Karim is one of seven kids and a recent graduate of law school. About two months ago he found a website about Christ and eventually was connected with my national friend who gave me his name and number. He had read much of the New Testament and spent many hours in conversation online with Christians.

He showed me around the city listing all the names of the roads we passed as if I was supposed to remember or care. The city is lacking of interesting tourist attractions so the road names made a nice substitute. I later realized the longer we walked that he really wanted to show me the old Catholic church left over from the occupation of France that was in shambles and another building belonging to the Catholic church. He stopped insisting on that when I told him I am not a Catholic and have little use for the Pope.

We found ourselves in a large park on a bench. I pulled out the Bible I had brought for him. He instructed nervously that I should put it in the newspaper to hide what we were reading. I spent about an hour answering his question from the Old Testament and New. Since he had never read the Old Testament, passages like Gen 3 and Isaiah 53 were surprising to him. He wanted to know "How do Christians pray? How do they fast? If I become a Christian do I have to go to church?" After our time in the park we went to a friends house whom he said is "open minded" like him. Together, the three of us toured the old medina and suq situated on the top of a large hill overlooking the city. The surroundings couldn't be more like Tacna, Peru unless it actually were. Crazy...if you've ever been to Tacna.

We hung out until about 12 pm when the next train was heading out. So after 8 straight hours together I learned a few things:

-I   need   to   learn   this   language   better!

-The best way to do so is just this: 8 hours with two guys who don't have a clue how to speak English or Spanish. -Both of their dads were Hajji's (they have traveled to Mecca, very serious Muslims). Growing up in strict Muslim homes they mocked a lot of things to do with Islam. I try to stay neutral and preach only Christ.
-They don't like to spend a lot of their time on the first visit talking about theology. Altogether we spent maybe 2 hours speaking about the Bible. The rest of the time we talked about my country and family, theirs, friends, food, everything. I asked him toward the end of the night, "No more questions?" He responded energetically, "Oh no! I have a ton. But next time." He even listed all his questions so I know he had some.

It reminded me of a time I sat down with a Kurdish family in Atlanta and opened my Bible and began to explain salvation after maybe fifteen minutes in his house. When I came up for breath after my forth point the Kurdish man asked, "Don't you want to ask me anything about myself?" It seems they don't like to get "straight to the point" like we yanks do. I will have to work on my relationship building skills.

After three different trains and interrupted sleep I returned back home at 8 am. 3 nights and 3 days total. I spent a total of $51. Traveled over 1,000 kilometers by train and taxi. I am definitely going to make this a monthly thing.

Talked to all three of my contacts on the phone as soon as I arrived back at my house at 8 am:

-Mohammed has read John 4 following up strong on his daily devos! -Ali had just woken up and was preparing to do his devotions since I had only left him the day before. (Seemed like a week) He had also already left a post on Gospel in China blog.

-Karim had begun reading Genesis and thought it was amazing how God made man in His image and breathed into him, a living soul. Pray for these guys as they are spread out over a 9-hour distance. Maybe we'll do a virtual church someday. MUST LEARN LANGUAGE!

Wives: Just Expensive?

My good friend Mark Tolson is getting married tomorrow to a wonderful young lady, Natasha Witt. That, along with the present absence of my wife has got me thinking. She has been gone since Monday. When she left with my mother-in-law I left on my trip. Since Monday I have spent a grand total of $62! $51 of that was on the three-day trip! Now I don't have the exact numbers but that doesn't even compare when my beautiful wife and two precious children are here. So, I was thinking, Mark Tolson, wives are expensive! And kids even more!

BUT

-I had a Peanut Butter and Honey sandwich for dinner tonight. Cheap pizza for dinner last night.
-Nobody wants to be held by me right now.
-I went into the kitchen to fix my PB&H sandwich and found my sons spoon in there from the last time I was feeding him PB right out of the can. Almost cried.
-Watched a movie by myself tonight (first time in years)
-Haven't gotten a kiss for 5 days and I'm going through withdrawal (the men do kiss on the cheek here so that is some consolation. I go out of the house just to "say hi" when I'm feeling lonely)
-The bird's and the bachelor have made a mess and...it's still a mess. (Thank God for house help coming tomorrow for $1/hour before the queen gets home!)
-I am listening to music, which I never do because this place is so quite it scares me
-and the list goes on and on and on and on

So to answer the question, "Just expensive?" Yes. But worth every penny and more!

Another Mid-Year Review
August 18

What have I learned about God?

-He will bring me low and desperate before he will raise me up. He wants me to hope only in Him. When the situation seems hopeless. He is faithful to shed light just where he knows I need it. He wants me to follow blindly. I am only now seeing glimpses of ministry and the church.

-He wants me to learn to stand against the flow, the popular opinion, the fear, the caution, the "elders", the devil and most of all my pride. My prayer is for God to use us here in a world-impacting way. I don't know how but God can! He wants to. I need to get out of his way.

What have I learned about the work?

Life is a constant pressure for those who will follow Christ. The nervousness I feel everyday as I witness for Christ here in this Muslim country must be swallowed up in faith. Rest must not come to this life long term. God will give periods of rest but life on the edge of danger was the life of every disciple of Christ. How much less my life?
The most important part of a disciple's life is his love for Christ. Our love for Christ can be measured against our love for ourselves. Anyone unwilling to suffer for Christ does not love Christ. My mission will be to grow disciples who love Christ above their own lives.

I never knew why Phil 1:21 was my life's verse growing up. It didn't seem to fit my life in American suburbs. Now I know why: it is to be my life's message. If I can have ten men on my team here who love nothing but Christ and hate nothing but the Devil, there will be nothing the Devil can do to stop the spread of salvation! I will always be glad I came to live among these people. A lifetime of ministry to a people must begin here no matter where God leads me later. I will know God's will by conviction not by popular opinion.

Category: "Things that make you sick"
One thing that makes you sick are rotten eggs. I learned this as my wife was away last week. I cooked one up for breakfast that had been sitting unattended for way to long. I have a horrible sense of smell so I fried it, ate it, and then...well you know what else. I've been "queasy" ever since.

Another little known cause of sickness is your common house fan.

That's right, fans. So the house church we are attending is usually full with around 20 to 25 people on any given Sunday. They close the windows during the singing and the singing can last up to an hour. So with no air circulation, 25 bodies, and 90+ degree temps, let's just say we're sweating. It is so miserable that it's hard to pay attention.

So, I went out last week and purchased the most powerful fan I could find and presented it proudly to the church as a gift! I thought everyone would be thrilled. Today as we started singing I had our high-powered, oscillating fan on the highest setting of 3 blowing equally on all 20 attendants and was enjoying it. No sweat dripping off my nose. Everybody's happy, right? NOPE. The guy sitting next to me reaches over and turns it OFF! I was in shock! What is this guy doing! He makes a motion to his lungs and says, "Sick, sick." So, not willing to bend so quickly I reach over and turn it back on to level 2. "Let's compromise." I offered. Our compromise ended up being level 1! Level one is the equivalent of a midget blowing through a straw! DIDN'T FEEL IT AT ALL! So there we sat all sweating just happy to have narrowly averted serious sickness. As soon as the service was over it was quickly turned off and everyone except the four foreigners present agreed that they may all be sick tomorrow due to my gift. Now I understand why all the taxis ride around with all their windows up and the knobs removed.

So, next time you are playing Scatagories and you come up with the category: "Things that make you sick" you can confidently write down: Fans (for "F"), wind (for "W"), or Ventilation (for "V").

Christians believe in God?

I went to lunch with Redouan the Muslim today. Redouan has been a good friend and great language helper. I've stayed the night at his family's house, camped out with him, and witnessed to him the whole time. He insists that a Muslim can't change and that I should stop talking about religion because it's dangerous. As we were eating some chicken and olives we sat there with three of his friends, Mohammed, Mohammed, and Mo...no, Samir. Chances are in any crowd that 50% are named Mohammed or some derivation of that.

I had never met his friends before. One works in Europe. The other two are in the army, one in the capital and one stationed in the far south. I also told them a little about myself. I have two kids and I always follow that by "alhamdulilah" or Thanks to God. When I said that, Redouan's friends turned to him and said, "Is he a Muslim." No". "But he said, 'Thanks to God.'" they insisted. "Right, well, he's a Christian and really believes in God." Redouan explained. "Well, he is named after a Muslim prophet, the brother of Moses." They insisted further. They looked confused so Redouan continued. "He believes in all the prophets, Noah, David, Adam, Jesus, he just doesn't believe in Mohammed. He's a good guy. He's not against the Muslims like the Jews are. You can trust him, he's just like a Muslim."

At least 200 times in my 200 days here I have had to explain, "Yes, my name is the name of a prophet (in Islam they are taught that all the prophets in the Old Testament were Muslim prophets. Adam was the first Muslim. Abraham was the father of Arab Muslims of whom Mohammed was a direct descent.). But Moses and his brother were actually Jews, not Muslims. So my name was originally Hebrew. But I am a Christian. I believe in God."

All of that is new for them. They usually just look at me, not agreeing but knowing they don't know enough to disagree. It was a funny feeling as I listened to Redouan explain to them who I am. Many Muslims like them around the world are unaware that a true Christian actually believes and loves God deeper than they do. They thought Christians are typically pagan people since I was the first believer in Christ that they had met.

That must be one of the greatest obstacles to the gospel in Muslim lands. To be a follower of Christ never cannot be a morally good thing in their minds because they don't know any real followers of Christ. They view Christians as the nominal Catholics they watch in Europe. In America if you tell someone you are a Christian and they assume, "Oh, you're one of those GOD people." Tell someone in a Muslim world that you are a Christian and they assume, "Oh, you don't believe in God."

Ishmael

I was at a bus station in Spain the other day by myself waiting. I always carry with me a few Jesus Films, New Testaments, stuff like that. A guy in a white Islamic robe sat next to me, pulled out his

Koran, and started reading. At the time he caught me in the spiritual activity of stuffing my face with a Turkish Shwarma. So God spoke right to me and I knew I had to let this fellow know that neither his skirt nor his Koran could intimidate a follower of Christ. Also, he has a soul that will spend the rest of eternity in hell with Mohammed. That is real. So before our bus pulled up I said in Arabic, "Since you like to read, why don't you read this?" and stuck out the Injeel (NT) to him. He smiled and looked at it and then back at me. Then said, "On the bus, we'll talk."

We didn't get the opportunity to sit together but he sat behind me. My seat was next to another Arab named Ishmael. As Ishmael and I began to talk he asked me if I pray. It's a funny question I think I have never heard asked to me sincerely until I arrived here. Since then I have been asked that maybe 50 times or more. That is how they judge your spirituality: prayer. Then they always want to know how much. 5 times/day? Less? They expect that I don't pray. They are shocked when I tell them more than 5 times/day.

Anyway, I was having a great time telling my friend Ishmael about how God loves us and wants to hear us talk to him. He wants that relationship with us. He wants, like a good father to answer our prayers. He has made a way for our sin to be removed so that our prayers actually reach the Holy of Holies! Our Islamic friend (and there is a difference between an Islamist and a Muslim) sitting behind us would stick his face through our seats and interrupt me every five seconds with Koranic dogma. Unwilling to talk interrupted I told him when he was done then we'd talk fair. eg. I talk you listen, then you talk I listen. Unwilling to actually listen he soon sat back and left Ishmael and me to our rational selves.

Ishmael claimed that being a good follower of the law ensured that his prayers were heard. I was able to show Ishmael through Romans 3 that I had just read that morning how the law was given only to show us that, well, we better shut our proud yapper! (It really says that, check it out!) We are under the law and condemned by it. We are in desperate need of Romans 4 grace! Ishmael was stunned by the new truth of the Word of God. As I switched buses he gave me his phone number and asked that I come and stay with his family next time I am through so we can talk more. He promised to read the New Testament that I gave him.

Language Note: Being on my 2nd language, words slosh around in my fairly hollow brain and switch compartments freely. As I disembarked the bus I explained to the bus driver how I had stayed on the bus too long and needed to get on another bus going to another city. After about 6 sentences he stopped me and said, "Look, I don't understand what you're saying." I laughed out loud and apologized when I realized that after about an hour and a half of uninterrupted Arabic with Ishmael I had just rattled all that off to my Spanish bus driving in Arabic. Today I totally forgot the simple Spanish word for "meanwhile" that I have used thousands of times. I had to ask the nearest Hispanic. I'm afraid my second language is giving way to the third.

Prayer Head Banging

On my first trip to Egypt I noticed that a number of older men who were more religious had a dark spot on their foreheads that looked like a bruise. Some were light and barely visible and other were dark, wrinkled, and well, fairly unattractive. Asking around I discovered that bruise was actually like a permanent rug burn from prayer. So when they pray and bow their heads to the ground they rub their foreheads on the carpet in order to obtain that spiritual rug burn.

I asked Mohammed, a local storeowner around the block from my house how he got his. He said, "I pray a lot." I asked him as well if did it on purpose. He denied that vehemently and claimed it was a result of such repetition that it could not be helped just as an athlete has permanent bruises or scars on their knees. Well, I didn't buy it.

When Jesus taught us to prayer, he taught from the point of how NOT to pray because the idea of prayer was set by the Pharisees. They were hypocrites in every way and Jesus condemned it. In EVERY point the Muslims transgress the teachings of Jesus on prayer:

Jesus said:

"And when thou prayest, thou shalt not be as the hypocrites are: for they love to pray standing in the synagogues"- Yep, Muslims. **"and in the corners of the streets"**- Yep, Muslims lay their prayer mat down and do their ostentatious ritual so everyone can see they are praying.

"use not vain repetitions"- Yep. Five times per day. The same written prayer for each time of day. Old men can be seen with a string of 33 prayer beads praying through the 99 names of God (in Islam). I've sat and counted one old man do go through that string more than 20 times in less than half and hour. VAIN repetitions.
"Do not sound a trumpet before thee, as the hypocrites do in the synagogues and in the streets, that they may have glory of men"- Call to prayer is universally called in the streets and everyone here knows who is going to pray and who isn't.
"Beware of the scribes, who desire to walk in long robes"- A "serious" Muslim has prescribed for him to wear long white or black robes on Friday as the day of prayer.
"for a shew make long prayers"- The longer the prayer in Islam the more reward is received.

It's amazing that after 2,000 years the Devil is still pulling the same tricks that he was on men back when Jesus instructed us how to pray and how NOT to pray. Here in North Africa I see every day and especially on Friday prayers that get no higher than the mosque's roof: Jesus said, "Verily I say unto you, They have their reward."

About those who desire praise before men in their worship before God, Jesus said:

"The same shall receive greater damnation."

We have come for the same reason Jesus did: to preach freedom and grace to a people under law and condemnation. Please pray for the 1.3 billion Muslim people who will suffer greater condemnation if they don't turn to the Lamb of God who takes away the sins of the world!

Evangelizing and Being Evangelized

I have found that one of the hardest things to do is to witness to someone while they are witnessing to you. As I write this, my wife is sitting with a friend, Hayet, at our dinner table being evangelized. This lady has been the most persistent at her efforts to make my wife a Muslim. Often I have been asked this questions, "Wash salmty?"

That means, literally, "Have you Muslim-ed?" It is usually asked by a very excited, smiling new acquaintance who realizes I am learning Arabic. Since Arabic is the language of the Koran and that is the only language the Koran is able to be understood in, anyone who learns Arabic MUST be a new Muslim! At least, that is what they are hoping.

Of all the world religions there are two that are classified as major "missionary" religions: Christianity and Islam. Christ's command to us is, "Go ye into ALL the world and preach the gospel". Mohamed commanded his followers, "Go into all the world and spread Islam by force if necessary."

Well, no one has forced us yet but here are some of the ways they have tried to convert us:

1. Trickery- This was the first way I was "evangelized" since I didn't speak enough Arabic to do it any other way. A few friends that I had made after about a month in the country were trying to teach me Arabic. We were in their office and I was surrounded by about five of them. I wanted to learn verb conjugation in past tense but they wanted to trick me into saying, "There is no God but Allah and Mohamed is his prophet." They said it over and over, louder and louder, and demanded I repeat. That in Islam is known as the Shahhada. If you say that (and believe it, which I guess they forgot) then you are a Muslim and all your previous sins are forgiven. When someone wants me to say that I love to shock them by saying, "I believe there is only one God and Mohamed was not his prophet." They almost can't take it. I don't know why but I get a certain entertainment out of watching their emotional reactions.

2. Bribery- This one is the funniest. I have received free haircuts when a barber thought that because I was listening to him tell me about Islam that I might convert. My wife was in the market with a friend and gathered a crowd by merely asking questions about Islam. The crowd was very hopeful that she might become a "Mohammedan". That day she ate Belgium chocolates and cashews, drank bottled water, and brought a new shirt home ALL for free! So, we are learning one thing: if we become Muslims we'll be set here for life. Sometimes I am tempted when my support is low. ha ha.

3. The "Everybody's Doing It" argument- This is the most common. My wife's friend, Hayet came over tonight armed with this strategy. She is claiming that she saw on news network Aljezeera that a lot of Americans are becoming Muslim, especially women. Basically implying that if my wife was interested, well, it's completely normal and acceptable. My wife of course busted her bubble when she informed Hayet that after 23 years in America she has yet to see an American born woman wearing a Muslim head covering. Hayet wasn't sure what to say about that. My wife was once set up by Khadija when they went to work out. After their workout Khadija had set up my wife with a lady who speaks English to witness to her. That went on for about an hour. Usually when I tell them that thousands of Muslims around the world have become Christian including in their country that cancels that argument and we can move on to other more honest ways of convincing each other.

4.The "Obvious Truth" Argument- This one completely denies logic. Talking with two Muslims last week I gave the 5 or 6 reasons I believe Jesus was the "last prophet". Then I asked them what proof Mohamed gave that he was the last prophet. They were mostly silent, quoted some verses from the Koran where Mohamed said he was the last prophet. So, I restate my question and they say, "Because he was the last prophet." That is about the answer I get from everybody who tries to defend Islam. It seems that there is no argument against blind statements.

5."The Koran Miracle"- They often think that if someone reads the Koran that they'll be enraptured by the beauty and truth of the Koran and become a Muslim. Only problem is when I read it is not so beautiful because it is not true. When I tell them I have already read the Koran and don't believe it is from God it causes mixed reactions. That's the major reason anyone coming to work with Muslims should read the Koran. Literally NO ONE here has ever read the life of Christ in the New Testament. Until your read the Koran they'll always be waiting for you to consider Islam before you can really know the truth. Once you've "considered Islam" and rejected it they are always very surprised and interested to know why. They believe that before Jesus Christ comes back to the earth a second time that the whole world will turn to Islam.

6. "Back to your roots"- Muslims believe that everyone is born Muslim and through time and environment are turned away from it by their weaknesses. So everyone since Adam has been Muslim at birth. To become Muslim is to "return" to Islam.

There are many more but these are some of the most common. What I or my wife have yet to encounter is a Muslim who can show us from the Koran why they are a Muslim and why we should be Muslims. What will make all the difference in the world for a Muslim who has blindly followed his religion is to read the truth of the Word of God. Please pray for the thousands of Muslims who will receive the "Message of Hope" being sent by volunteers this week.

Ramadan: Not good for the naturally ugly

Ramadan is coming up in a couple weeks. For those of you unfamiliar with Ramadan it is the most spiritual event on the calendar of the Muslims every year. For one solid month (and those dates change every year according to the lunar calendar) the Muslims will fast from food, water, sin, and pleasure during the daylight hours. As soon as the evening call the prayer is sounded they are off to the races. A feast of food is preceded by everything they had abstained from during the day.

One comical point of Ramadan is it is a "Hashuma" (shame) for a woman to wear makeup during daylight. Why? Well, to wear makeup may make a woman pretty. OK? So? Well, if she is pretty she may attract the lust of a man. And that, is a sin they cannot afford on Ramadan since righteousness during Ramadan is worth hundreds more "heaven points" (those points that if you accumulate enough will buy your way into heaven) than any regular day. Since woman can't wear makeup during this time the naturally ugly can't leave their homes! That's right. Did you ever wonder what your girlfriend looks like without makeup? Well, if she's real ugly underneath there, she won't go anywhere during daylight hours. Now, as evening appears she'll have out the putty knife putting on her mask ready to go out on the town after dark. Pretty righteous, huh? Well, fortunately my wife is naturally beautiful and doesn't need makeup!

Ramadan will begin in less than two weeks. Please pray for the 1.3 billion blind Muslims during this time!

69

Mid-Shaban is here!

My wife noticed today that our baby sitter, Fatima, was not eating. She asked her why and she told her that it is Nus Sha'aban. "Nus" means "half" and "sha'aban" is the name of this month, the month before Ramadan. Next month, Ramadan is the month of God in Islam so this month is the month of the people. So after digging around we discovered from her and other Muslims and ex-muslims the significance of this day:

-It is 15 days now until Ramadan starts

-Today the angels that sit on both your shoulders and write down all the good and bad you do, will take that report to God in heaven (I guess that means it'd be a good opportunity to take advantage of their absence!)

-Tonight after sunset God is said (in some Hadiths that the experts argue about their authenticity) to hand to the angels the fate of all humans for the coming year: who will die, who will marry, who will find a job, etc. Everything is determined tonight.

-Fasting today is optional yet desirable (unlike Ramadan when it will be obligatory). To fast today you may procure yourself a better year this coming year.

So after interviewing about ten muslims and an ex-muslim this is what I have found:

-Only the SERIOUS fast today. Fatima was the only one we could find fasting. Others said they forgot, others that they just didn't want to because they don't have to.

-Nobody knows what the origin of the teaching of this day is. A couple admitted it is just old tradition.

-Some say that God saved Noah from the flood on this day, other say Mohammed visited a special grave site, and a few other things.

-These days are good opportunities to teach people what Jesus said about fasting. I was able to tell a couple Muslim acquaintances I had just met all about what Jesus said about fasting and instances from my life.

Pray for Bilal, Fatima, Mustapha, and a ton of other Muslims we are witnessing to. Pray that Ramadan will be our opportunity to witness to them and they will open up to God's Word.

Totally Unlovable

I was paying for the rent on our office space today. My friend Said and I walked into the office of our landlord, who has just arrived by from Hajj (The Pilgrimage to Mecca, Saudi Arabia), and said hello or in Arabic "asalam ualaykum". Immediately a man in the office asked me if I was a Muslim. I said no and he proceeded to tell me that I have no right then to say "asalam ualaykum", which means "Peace to you". It made Said mad and they yelled at each other for about ten to fifteen minutes. The man told him that Muslims are the only ones with God so they are they the only ones with peace. The "prophet" Mohamed wrote in the Koran that if anyone says "peace" or "salam" to a Jew or a Christian on accident that they should immediately go to him and demand his "salam" back.

Islam is a religion of peace...only if everyone is Muslim. They are forbidden by their prophet to be at peace with any non-muslim. Thankfully after seven months here this is my first experience with someone who would not even say "salam" to me. But I have to admit, it made me mad. I was offended. Nobody likes it when someone can't even be nice. The dude was seriously hard to look at with the love of Christ.

So of all the people in the world Muslims seem to me to be the hardest to love. Of all the Muslims, the Arabs rank #1 on the "Hardest to Love List". After all they are so proud to of their prophet, their language, etc. Only North Korea could equal Saudi Arabia's intolerance for the Word of God.

So how do you love those who are so unlovable?

I always think about this guy I heard about who God calls his "enemy". This guy doesn't look for God and he doesn't understand or want to understand God. He leads others astray with his pride. He won't humble himself at all and loves himself much more than he loves God. He is a liar, hateful, jealous, idolater, and a rejecter of truth. The list could go on and on. Then I remember that this enemy of God...was me.

I owe the Muslims a debt. Why? Well, I grew up in a Christian country and in a Christian family in a Christian church reading the Christian book. I heard and they didn't. That means, I am a debtor to those who haven't got the truth. There are 1.3 billion Muslims and

71

most have no opportunity to hear and search in the Word of God. Please pray for laborers.

South Koreans Apologize

Today I read in <u>Fox News</u> that the remaining nineteen South Koreans that were taken captive by the Taliban were released last week. The team of South Koreans were on a medical trip providing relief to those impacted by the war. Two were tragically executed and two were released the week before. We were praying for their church, their families, and their courage during this very trying time. The real surprise to me was who ended up being the ones apologizing. After risking and giving their lives to bring medical aid to this war torn Muslim country it was the South Korean Christians who were being criticized by their own country for even going there!

The South Koreans and their church apologized for going there and putting themselves in danger. I don't know many who would have the guts to go to Afghanistan right now to be a witness for Christ. The South Koreans are known all over Asia and Africa as being the bravest witness in the world for Christ. It is sad to see them apologizing after risking their lives and even two of them giving their lives to share Christ's message just as he commanded.

September

Life on the Farm...for Jesus

As part of our language learning, our team is taking 3 days of the month to separate and travel to different parts of the country and stay in homes of the North Africans. It is always an intense time of language learning. You can't escape into a book. You just have to talk.

I went back where I had gone on my first trip when I was alone but took the family this time. We visited Mohammed who has recently accepted Christ. He was happy to see us as always and the kids loved the farm. They rode a donkey (not willingly), I helped build a cement wall, we hiked along a dried up creek bed, witnessed to a couple of the workers on their farm, took his pregnant sister a half hour away to the city for a doctors visit, and ate a TON of food fresh from the farm. For 3 days and two nights we had no running water. My wife loved that! We slept on the cement roof of their house under the stars on foam cushions. One night as we lay there talking we counted ten shooting/falling stars (my wife tells me that there is a difference.) Since the house didn't have any doors yet (they are working on that) we changed clothes on the roof, too.

Mohammed has been struggling in his new Christian walk. After accepting Christ I immediately saw him witness to others about Christ. Then he went home and everything changed. We are always more courageous to tell strangers about Christ than our families. It may help you to know a little about his family.

His grandpa on his dad's side had two wives who gave birth to twenty-four kids, six of whom have passed away! His grandpa on his mom's side had six kids. So he has twenty-three living aunts and uncles! He has over 100 cousins! Sheesh. I have ten! Anyway, he is related to pretty much everyone who lives within a half an hour. They are all Muslim except for an uncle who never told him he was a Christian until after Mohammed accepted Christ.

Surrounded by that situation he gets a little discouraged. He had only read five chapters in John since I was there last, three weeks ago. So for two mornings we woke up early and read John 9 and 10. He wrote down what he got out of it and is hopefully continuing. No, wait. I was under conviction after writing that line so I called him and he has read John 11. We praise the Lord for the opportunity to encourage him. I left him one Jesus film. His goal is to tell one of his 100 cousins about Christ and give him the film. That's for starters. It could blow up in his face and get him in quite a bit of trouble but hey, that's why Christ came, right? To bring a sword? That's what he said! Check it out if you don't believe me.

Pray for Mohammed's family. We hope to make an impact on them by our testimony while we lived with them so that when they find out he's a Christian, they might accept that as a good thing. We didn't get into a lot of the Bible while we were there. Just tried to share our lives with them and be a blessing to them. We prayed and asked God to bless their family in the name of Jesus Christ with them. Next month I'll be returning with 20 kilos of Mildew Medicine for their grapes. His dad hugs me and kisses me every time I talk about bringing that medicine.

There is NO love in their home. Mom and dad sleep in separate rooms like EVERY other home I have been in here. (I am still wondering how Mohammed, his two siblings, and their 100 cousins all got here.) Not a lot of smiles going on. No joy at all. Especially pray for Mohammed's little brother. He is only twelve and Mohammed is his hero. Hopefully he will be one to follow Mohammed's example.

Four Crazy Years!

Today is our forth Anniversary. That's right, four big ones! Many of you may not know my wife well so let me tell you a little bit about what she has meant to me over the last four crazy years:

-She had the courage to marry a passionate but often brainless young man on his way OUT of the country.
-She traveled all across the country and listened to the exact same five sermons for the first ten months of our marriage including one trip to California and back when she was seven months pregnant.
-She helped me put together the first, second, and third Baptist Camp for World Evangelism where many college students committed their lives to be missionaries.

-She flew with her four week old son to Peru and left him when he was six weeks old at home for four hours per day while we studied Spanish.

-We enjoyed our first and second anniversary in Peru where she learned Spanish and loved the people there.

-She encouraged my faith and discouraged my fears when I started praying about coming to the Muslim world. She was always ready to be way out of her comfort zone (which is much smaller for a woman than for a man) for Jesus.

-She lived our third year together in the US where she helped start an outreach in Atlanta to Muslims. The first Muslim to accept Christ was a young girl named Shayma that she led to Christ.

-She is diligently going through language school AGAIN with two kids now!

-Through it all she has remained beautiful, resourceful, and just plain lovely.
-Now on our forth anniversary she is running her first ladies meeting with ex-Muslim converts to Christ while I am working in the office till 7 pm. Most wives I know wouldn't stand for that. (Don't worry. We are celebrating tomorrow!)

Three continents, three languages, two kids, and four years later I can say she is exactly what every missionary wife ought to be. I love you, babe!

The Point System I learned something from Abdel Salam, the farm hand at Mohammed's house, that I have been investigating the last few days. While witnessing to him he mentioned to me that the prayers on Friday were "worth" seventy times more than a simple, normal prayer. "Seventy!" I exclaimed, surprised by his exactness at the worth of such an intangible item. So I have been asking a ton of Muslims since that time and this is what I have found:

-The word "Ajar" translated from the idea of payment or recompense from God is a measurable amount in Islam. That is the same word

Jesus used when speaking of the Pharisees when he said, "They have their reward." I'll just call them "Rewards" or "points" here though they call them "Ajar."

-The basic unit of a point is a single prayer performed by a single person by himself or herself not in a mosque. That is worth one point.

-A prayer in a mosque is worth 27 points (or 27 times that of a prayer in your home).

-Fasting in Ramadan is worth so much (nobody knows exactly how much) that it makes up for the whole year of missed prayers.

-The last ten days of Ramadan are worth the most.

-Prayers on Fridays are worth a "LOT" more points than on other days. The earlier you arrive at the mosque the more points you get. The later you arrive the less points. God hears the prayers of those in the front row better than those in the back rows. (I am not joking.)

-Prayers on "Laila el-Qadr" are worth that of 1,000 months.

-If you do any of the following while at the mosque you completely lose your points:
pass gas, look at a woman, talk during the preaching (even if your asking "what in the world did that guy just say!?"), burp (any bodily functions, really), step on dirt, etc

-If you loan someone money without interest, let's say 100 bucks and they don't pay you back for 10 days you get 100 points for everyday they don't pay you back. So that'd be 1,000 points for all you math wiz's out there. That is "Sadaqa" or giving.

-There are many more, which I have not yet found out but you get the basic idea. You'd think that since they have gone to the trouble to figure out what is worth more and less that some accountant minded Muslim would make a business of tabulating a persons "points" at the end of each fiscal year. Like an H & R Block for the soul. That way they'd know how many points they have to play around with on the "sin" end of the balance. However, no one keeps track because only God knows the total of sin and righteousness that each person has. They hope their balance tips in their favor. The only crazy thing is, they still believe that God is sovereign and will forgive who he will. So he can still decide not to forgive you if you have worked hard building up points or on the flip side, he can decide to forgive a pointless wonder like myself!

-Islam is a religion of laws and balances like every other false religion in the world that tries to give man salvation through his good deeds. All our good deeds, however, are as filthy as disease laden, puss rags.

Their carnal minds will not understand the grace of Christ and the love of God alone. We must have the Holy Spirit's help. Pray with me during the beginning of Ramadan next week for these Muslims to understand Christ's message.

Looking Around the Room

So what does the church look like that we go to on Sundays? The building is just another cement house on the block. No one knows it's a church except the people that have been on the inside and have seen all the Bibles, hymn books, and Christians. There is a pulpit. Everyone sits on the traditional couches that line the wall. It has capacity space of maybe 30. So it's usually full most Sundays. But, that's not what a church is. A church is the people. So here is a quick snap shot of who was in the room yesterday:

The Construction worker- Ahmed is 33 and is from the south of the country. He is the darkest guy in the room. He first heard the gospel through radio a couple of years ago. He moved up here maybe two months ago and got a construction job. He is always smiling and is excited about being a Christian. His whole family knows he is a believer. He has a simple, courageous way about him. He is a lot of fun.

The Old Christian- Said is around 40. He is the oldest Christian in the group. He is single. He accepted Christ through a Christian ministry in Europe that rehabilitates drunks and drug addicts.

The Dad- Abdlallah is around 45 and has been saved for more than five years. His wife is not yet a believer so he and his 16-year-old son (who is also a believer) come alone. Though he's been saved for a while he never grew because he never got into a church. He has been at the church now for around two months and is growing. I had to help him find Isaiah yesterday to give you an idea. His son is an awesome kid. He is the ONLY Christian teenager I know in this country (there are others, I am sure. I just don't know them.)

The Church-planter- Bob is the white guy in the group. They have been here for over 20 years with a dream to plant this church! He has been faithful. He and his wife both speak Arabic very well. His wife plays the guitar like no other fifty-year-old woman I have ever seen. They love the people and are excited that the church is growing. He is the only foreigner who has helped me get involved in the church.

The Pastor- Layman is in his mid thirties with two kids. Bob won him and trained him. His wife is still not a believer, which is a real weight on him. He prays like a North Carolinian camp meet-er: loud. He sweats a lot so if you come don't sit close to him in the summer. He is super involved in online evangelism and follow-up of radio and TV.

The Ladies Section- The ladies all sit separate from the men. Not because they have to, just because the service starts after everyone has fellowshipped and that usually segregates the ladies and men. There were five of them yesterday. Only two were married. I don't know a ton about them. I'll have to get my lovely wife to post on this one.

The young married couple- Rahim is about twenty-six and newly married. His wife is expecting actually. Bob won him to the Lord and then he won his then girlfriend. He's a great guy though unemployed. He sings with real passion and loves to pray. He's been saved about two years maybe. His wife still wears a head covering because she finds it easier than telling her family she is a believer. Some are courageous and some not so much.

The unbeliever- Mohammed was there yesterday. He is an older man who has spent most of his life in prison for political dissent. His son is just one month old and is dying from kidney failure. He has been the last three weeks because Bob had been witnessing to him and invited him. He brought his wife and baby today. The doctors here don't have the ability to help this little baby. They are trying to get the baby to Europe but I don't see it happening. The baby is bloated, as his abdomen has filled with fluid. It was heartbreaking to hold that little baby knowing, that unless God does a miracle, he will be dead in a few months. The church isn't super open to unbelievers attending. They prefer that everyone do witnessing on their own time and once someone accepts Christ, then they are invited.

The Guy in the wheel chair- Hamid was born with deformities to his body that have left him in a wheelchair. About fourteen years ago a French believer started coming down here on vacation and witnessing to him. Just five years ago he finally accepted Christ as his Savior. He is the church poet. Every week he writes a poem and reads it to the church.

Those are most of the regulars. Which is a great growth considering five months ago the crowd was about half that size. So that is a look around   the   room.

They sing loud. They pray with passion. Yesterday was dedicated to prayer for freedom. We prayed that God would give the Christians freedom to meet under the law. Please pray with us.

Sundays

It just dawned on me that many of you may not know what a Sunday looks like for a new missionary in a Muslim country. Maybe you are like me, in that you go to church every Sunday, twice, and then once during the week. A Sunday consists of fighting with the kids and wife to get out of the door on time, maybe a bus route, Sunday school, church, lunch at Appleby's or Cracker Barrel, a nap (if you're the preacher, final preparation for the evening service), finally the evening service, fellowship with a few friends out of the hundreds who showed up for church, and then home again. It's hard to know what's normal but that's my best guess.

Sunday was the most challenging day of the week spiritually for us when we first arrived. There were two national Christians we met when we first got here who gathered sometimes with a couple others on Sundays. Only problem is we weren't invited. I know, I asked, and we weren't. So we were stuck without any believers to fellowship with on Sunday or any day for that matter. Now after almost eight months here on the ground in language school this is what our day was like yesterday:

We spent the morning at home preparing for the afternoon. I studied I Corinthians 1. One chapter usually takes me about an hour to get every word. My wife took care of the kids while I reviewed the lesson I was going to be teaching in the afternoon.

At 1 pm I and the family met our coworker and his wife at our meeting place. We didn't walk between any big white pillars nor underneath a tall steeple like I did when I was a kid. I never understood the steeple anyway. We were gathering to hold a cyber Bible study. After about an hour of technical difficulties we finally got on the webcam with Ali (connecting from five hours away, he is the twenty one year old Christian I wrote about earlier who had never been to a church service when I met him after trusting Christ more than one year ago) and Karim (connecting from six hours away, he is a twenty four year old, unemployed, law grad who I met about a month ago).

Since Ramadan is starting this Thursday I was answering a question asked earlier by Karim, "How do Christian's fast?" We looked at fasting from the lives of Daniel, David, Jesus Christ, and the first church. Muslims fast to get points for heaven. Christians fast to get close to God when needing some serious miracles from heaven.

We wrapped up the meeting around 3:30 after prayer and singing. From there we all packed in my car and headed out for the next service, which was to start at 5 pm. The closest church we could find that opened their doors to us is a little over an hour away. I give serious praise to God for them. When other churches were too afraid to allow us to come they accepted us with wide-open arms. Our road takes us over a mountain range to a city of over half a million people just on the other side. The road is two lanes almost the whole way. So even though its only about seventy kilometers it takes over an hour. The mountains are beautiful, especially when there is rain, which there hasn't been for over four months.

We picked up Ahmed en route and arrived just before 5 pm. There were twenty-three people there in total: nine foreigners and fifteen nationals. We prayed and sang to the Lord for close to an hour. They do this part of the service with the windows closed though it is still audible on the street outside. The pastor preached about the holiness of God from Isaiah 6 and how Christ is our holiness. After the service we hung out talking until around 8 pm. The pastor asked me to preach the sermon next week before we left. I am sure I am not ready for that...but we'll give it a shot. On the road back we about died twice. Crowded two lane roads in the mountains are bad for that.

So that was my Sunday. It is not what we want it to be but we thank God for it today. We were able to teach a little of the Word of God in Arabic and hopefully be a blessing to the believers we met with for church. Our dream is to see thousands of new believers meeting in homes being led by national pastors that we had a part in training. For those who have no access to a church, we dream of connecting hundreds of new believers to the Word of God through an interactive video church like we did with Ali and Karim.

But until then, that was our Sunday.

Rah Rah Rah!   Today is going to be an honest post. Not complaining, I hope, but honest.

I thought about not writing anything today. I scanned all the victories on my friends' blogs from around the world and those I have never met and just decided that my day... well, stunk. So I was just going to keep all that to myself. But after thinking about it, I think it would be dishonest to write about all the victories and all the good times and none of the discouragements. You wouldn't really understand what ministry to Muslims is like if I don't talk about all of it.

Language school to begin with can be a spiritually low time. Your primary focus isn't ministering the Word but just learning how to talk. This being the second (and last, Lord willing) time that I am going through language school it is getting tedious. I get easily frustrated when I read blogs of people actually spending their time on ministry.

After morning language school I spent over an hour meeting and witnessing to two guys. It was all the same old stuff. "Have you become a Muslim yet?" "Jesus wasn't the Son of God. God doesn't have sons." "Jesus didn't die on the cross. Mohamed said so." I try to get in enough gospel so they could respond if they ever want to do so in the future. I left wondering what I often wonder on days like this:

"Does God hate Arab Muslims?"
"Should we be wasting any time and money on Muslims?"
"Would God be mad at me when I get to heaven if I decide to be a Calvinist?"
"That youth pastor position is looking pretty good right now."

I would never write this in a prayer letter. Luckily, prayer letters come out once per month. Something good is bound to happen in a month that I can write about. But when I write on a blog everyday I have to choose to skip days or to be honest.

So those are the real thoughts that the devil throws at me, just so you know. So what are God's thoughts:

"He doesn't want any to perish."
"My job is the process. God's job is the product."
"God loves me and is proud of me...no matter what."
"The flywheel is going to start turning some day. The gold is just a few more dynamite blasts away. Must keep working."
"The leanest and hardest times are the 'before' picture. The times of blessings are the 'after'. No 'after' pictures without 'before' pictures. So I need to trust God and look with expectation to the future."

Now...I'll just keep saying that to myself. If you find yourself in a rough spot...just keep thinking on "these things."

A Sunday during Ramadan

I am sitting at my house at 10 pm after a satisfying day. No one was saved but there was progress.

The church service, which usually starts in the late afternoon, started at noon today. It is starting early for Ramadan. Around 6:30 pm the streets are empty, and I mean empty. Almost everyone fasts all day and then gather in their homes to break the fast at sunset during this 30-day month. As soon as the call to prayer is made everyone eats one date, takes a drink of milk, and goes to pray. Muslims were told by Mohamed in the Koran to break the fast with dates and milk so they continue that tradition until today. Next week we are scheduled to have the evening meal at two families homes. I guess we just won't be as hungry as they will be. Typically they eat all their traditional foods: Harira (a soup with meat, tiny noodles, tomatoes, etc that they eat all over the Muslim world), taijin, many different types of bread, spoof (almond mixture), shberkia (a cookie covered in honey), boiled eggs...you get the idea.

Anyway, I told you that the church met early because all Christians still belong to Muslim families. So if they didn't show up for the meal it would be like not showing up at home for thanksgiving or Christmas morning. Most of their families know that they are Christians. So they don't pray but they show up for the feast. It is a very uncomfortable time for the Christians that require them to take a stronger stand for Christ.

Last week they asked me to preach the main message. Since the service goes for sometimes 2 hours there might be other short messages. This time I was the main event. I was pretty nervous about it. In the end it turned out all right, I hope. I preached from the book of Acts. Acts was the second book in the Bible that I read in Arabic so thus, most of my lessons I have preached here come for Acts and John. It was really a big milestone for me. I have preached at meetings I have organized and recruited for but those are easy because those people had never heard any other sermons. These people I preached to today, though, meet twice a week for preaching. They have an Arab pastor and he's a fireball pray-er and preacher. Those who have visited us know what I mean. Bro. Gardner says Tony Howeth used to pray like that...before he lost the Holy Spirit I guess.

After arriving home from that meeting at 5 pm, I had dinner with the family and back to our meeting place for another Bible study at 6:30. We met with two guys who are really searching for the truth. That is strange but these are the ONLY two guys I have met here that are so far away from their Muslim God that they don't do Ramadan. So I drove through a ghost town to our meeting place and as over 1 million Muslim broke their fast and prayed in the name of Mohamed... we had a Bible study!

These guys have both been to our Bible studies before. Typically

83

what I do when we have a Bible study is hit a quick one-liner that presents them the gospel in 45 minutes or less. I guess because I am #1 Afraid I'll never get a shot with those present again and/or #2 hoping to see if they will get an epiphany and accept Christ as their Savior on the spot. Here are some of my One-shot-accept-or-reject-it sermons:

-Ye must be born again
-Jesus-the second Adam
-The forgiveness of Jesus
-The Resurrection
-The Crucifixion proof in the Old Testament
-Being a Son of God
-The prodigal son

All were structured to get a response on the first shot. But it has never happened. Usually it is met with one of two responses: #1: A blank stare. Usually meaning they have no idea how to filter what I just said into their Muslim brains. #2: A push back. Usually like my sister used to fight with me: yes huh, no, yes huh, no, yes huh, etc. Just a blunt denial of what I just said. "No, Jesus didn't die. No, Jesus is not the Son of God." Neither one of those responses get me anywhere.

So these two guys have a different response: They come back. They just haven't bought into anything I have been saying. (Maybe it is my Arabic.) So when we met tonight I really had no idea what to tell them. I mean, I have presented the plan of salvation to them multiple times. They LIKE it but don't ACCEPT it in their lives. So what do you do with someone who LIKES it. As we sat down and prayed together I asked God to show me what to say to them. He didn't say anything to me. So, I asked them, "You've been reading the Bible, right? Any questions?" They didn't say anything either. Just a look that said, "Teach us."

So I got down the white board and started drawing. In one hour I drew the history of the Bible. 66 books. 40 authors. Old Testament. Moses. The law. The prophets. The New Testament. Everything. They lit up. They learned something that is starting to connect the dots of all the things I have said. We ended the study with a reading of Isaiah 53 to connect the Old and New Testament in their minds. I think what I needed to do is put up a whole new structure for which they can hand these teachings on since their only current structure is the confusion of the Koran.

On the way home around 8 pm one of them said, "So Moses was the first to write. He wrote the first five books of the law. Then came twelve books of the history of Israel. Then five books by David. (I had to correct him there.) Then five Major Prophets. Then twelve Minor Prophets. All pointing to Jesus who Matthew, Mark, Luke, and John wrote about. Right?" Yeah, right. It was good to know someone was listening. I remember studying for a test on that in Bible College. This guy got it in just a few minutes.

So they both left excited about reading the Old Testament. We are still working at how to get the gospel across to their hearts so pray for us on that.

On a side note: I totally missed the Bengals game today. Turns out they lost 45-51 to the Browns!

Richard Wurmbrand
Just got finished reading a MUST READ!!!

Tortured for Christ by Richard Wurmbrand

The stories of bravery for Christ are amazing. Those men and women of God did not fear torture or their families reproach...they feared shame before Christ. They loved their Savior more than family, lands, comfort, and their very lives. If we had Christians like them today in North Africa the prisons would either be full of Christians preaching of the cross or there would be religious freedom. Indifference would NOT be an option as it is today.

With all are hearts we desire to see God put a fire of the gospel in the hearts and mouths of thousands of ex-Muslims all over the world but especially in North Africa who fear nothing but God and love Christ with a reckless abandon. (And yes, if you really love Christ like you should, people will accuse you of being reckless.)

From Sufi Islam to Christ

So, about the Lord being faithful. I have written about my friend Redouan the Agnostic before. He is an energetic guy who loves to talk a lot more than listen. But if I wait him out he is usually quite teachable. After I had only been here two months I gave Redouan a New Testament. He has been the most common face at our Bible studies and is always talking to me about people who want to meet us. He has brought two visitors himself who also don't believe in God. It seems that these people are connected here.

Redouan, despite all that, has been like the young ruler that Christ spoke to: he has believed it all but his heart desires his sin more. He often says, "When I get married and have kids I will become a Christian like you."

Today he came over to the office and was loaded with questions about the book of the Revelation of John. He stayed for about 3 hours and we attempted to answer these questions:

-What do I have to do after I become a Christian? What are the requirements in this club?
-Why did the angel speak so harshly to the seven churches if Jesus is all about love and grace?
-What does it mean I can "Die with Christ and live unto God"?

So we had a great time answering these from all over the Bible. Here is something amazing that I learned from Redouan.

Redouan's dad left his family a long time ago. Because of that he has always been looking for a place to belong. A few years ago he got involved with a sect of Islam called Sufi. Sufism is typified by a spiritual interpretation of the Koran. He said he would be required to wear a white robe and sit in a room for ten days straight listening to the Koran. He has the whole thing memorized. They would sleep in that room and learn from the preacher there. The preacher claimed to be the spirit of Mohammed sent as a messenger to man. Like a pope claims to be the "Vicar of Christ." So after they told him the dues for the group is $6 a month he wanted out. After ten days in that room he told them he wanted to go home. He was told he couldn't. So he said that as everyone slept he put on his shoes like he was going to the restroom and made a break for it. My coworker, Cesar, and I were cracking up imagining the scene he was describing.

Ever since that radical Muslim experience he has turned away from Islam though he says he still can't get all that Koran he memorized out of his head. Pray for him to accept Christ accept Christ as his Savior.

Mass Media

We are sure of one thing about ministry in Muslim countries: mass media is not just an option, it is necessary. To reach Muslims we need to witness to thousands to find one who is open to the message of Christ. To reach thousands by witnessing one on one is more than difficult. So we must use every media outlet that exists. I am convinced that their are new or "almost" new Christians all over North Africa and the Muslim world who are responding to these outlets and waiting for someone to help them in their walk with God. That is what I have found here. We desperately need a Web designer who is willing to learn Arabic.

We will also need teams on the ground all over the Muslim world to follow-up on contacts like we are and will be doing here: discipling them, forming churches, and finding the young men to train for leadership. The job is hard. The devil is against it. God wills it.

Missions and American Foreign Policy

Usually I wait until writing a post to name it but this one was easy. I have been asking you all to pray for Munir. He is teaching us Arabic for the next two weeks until a more permanent replacement arrives. Munir like all North Africans watches Al Jazeera News Network. So it's no surprise that they would have a very slanted idea of what goes on in Iraq. Much like many Americans who would watch too much CNN. Now you have to understand that North Africa speaks Arabic. While they aren't all Arabs, they still speak Arabic. The minority of North Africa is Arab. They are mostly indigenous people however the lines are very mixed and you can't tell one from the other without asking. Now, that said, Iraq is Arab. So they have a brotherhood. When we, the Americans, entered into Iraq there were protests all over the Arab world. Of course, they felt weak as we entered into their brother's home, tied up their president, and subdued the government. Did it need to happen? Sure. But you can understand their natural resistance to the whole thing.

Well in class the other day Munir asked me, "What do you think about the war in Iraq?" That is a horrible question for which honesty creates a huge argument and a non-response makes me feel like a coward. So I tried to answer it diplomatically but I soon found out that he wasn't near as interested in my opinion as he was his own opinion. So this is what he got out over the next 30 minutes or so:

-Iraq was a normal country with normal problems till we went in and messed it all up
-Our soldiers kill babies and woman by the scores.
-We are creating terrorists where before none existed.

So those things make me a little irritated because they are at the least ill informed. Especially when I have a brother in Iraq and a brother-in-law in Afghanistan. So I learned a long time ago that I am here on Christ's mission of the gospel. I cannot cheapen that message by alienating anyone fighting a political battle. So this is how I handled it:

-Establish the fact that Sadam was a murderous lunatic who needed to be taken out.
-Make him apologize for saying Bush should be executed
-Then...
"Listen Munir, those are some big problems in the world. But the truth is those are comfortable problems to discuss for you. You know why? Because you'll never be able to do anything about them. Do you know the problems you don't want to talk about? The kids on the street who don't have a home or food to eat and the handicapped people who hobble around all day. You don't want to talk about those problems because those are in your power to fix. What do you say we talk about those problems."?

I saw his countenance immediately change as we began to make a list of the problems we see around us everyday. Then we brainstormed about how we could help poor people eat who have no food. Then today we went to two foundations in town that deal with those problems to see how we could help. One was a home for 40 handicapped kids. We greeted all the kids and I really think he enjoyed   it.

We are going to keep looking for what we can do to help the street kids. There are literally hundreds of kids without homes who beg on the streets everyday. Always breaks my heart. So, that would be my advise for how to diffuse a useless discussion about American Foreign Policy.

I asked Munir today if he would go to hell for his sins. He said, "God knows." That is ALWAYS their response. They believe we cannot know how God will judge us. I told him that is the difference: The Christian knows what God will do because he told us in his Word. Again I talked with him about how Christ's blood cleanses us from all sin. His response was, "You know, you and me talk about religion a lot." Keep praying for him please.

In Burkina Faso

I am here in Burkina Faso now with my good friend and man of God Keith Shumaker. I am really burdened by the needs of this country and it's neighbors to the north. I want to ask you to pray with me for some serious laborers to be sent to Burkina Faso (50% Muslim) and Mali (90% Muslim) over the next year from America and Latin America. The doors are wide open to preach the gospel and start churches amongst Muslims.

So what am I doing here?

Well, there are around forty pastors from Togo, Ghana, Ivory Coast, and Burkina that have come together for this meeting organized by Steve Volante. About seven of them are former Muslims. I have been getting to know them by name and hear their stories. It has been a blessing. Today I was able to challenge them about the need of the Muslims. In Africa the Christian population has a lot of fear and prejudiced against their Muslim countrymen. And vice versa.

One pastor from the Southern part of Ivory Coast told me that after the civil war broke out in his country in 2002, sparked by the Muslim rebels in the northern part of the country, he had let hatred build up in his heart toward the Muslims and even said that he will never go up to the north. He told me that he had asked God to forgive him for that hatred. Hopefully he will have an active part in evangelizing the Muslims in the North of his country.

There are many other stories that I could tell you that God is doing with Keith here. God is using him greatly and will do a lasting work through him. He is sacrificial and full of love for all Africans.

Witch doctors in Islam

Last night before I preached a young lady came to the meeting. She told her story to a pastor from Togo that is visiting this week. She said that she was raised in a Muslim family. Recently some money was stolen out of her families home. Her parents went to a Muslim witch doctor to find some special revelation about who the thief was. The witch doctor fingered her as the perpetrator. She told the pastor that she didn't do it and knew from then on that her religion was false. So last night after seeing the Jesus video and hearing the sermon she accepted Christ as Savior.

We are praying for her and ask you to do the same. I hope she returns to the church service on Sunday. We'll hopefully get to know her more and share the gospel further.

Salif's Testimony

Salif was born and raised in a small village in Burkina Faso close to the Mali border. All of his village was Muslim and his dad was an Imam (Muslim preacher). When he was 6 years old his dad sent him to the Koranic school in Mali to learn to be an Imam. Mali is 92% Muslim and Burkina only 50%. In school Salif learned to memorize the Koran and all the prayers but didn't know what any of it meant. He was told that he could not learn the meaning until after he had performed his sacrifice. After graduation from school Salif had the responsibility to hold a sacrifice for his whole village in honor of his own graduation. So, he not having any money, went to the Ivory Coast to work. Not finding work he became the Imam for a village outside the city of Divo. He said, "Muslims respected me a lot for teaching them to memorize the Koran in Arabic so I ate a lot of chicken while I was an Imam." During Ramadan Salif would lead the "faithful" in prayers and recitation of the Koran. He saw so much hypocrisy in Islam that he decided to leave. He said everyone would pray during Ramadan and leave the Mosque empty the rest of the year.

Eventually he found himself as the guard for missionary Keith Shumaker. He was told by other Africans that if he was going to be a guard for a missionary that he would have to be a Christian. So he almost quit. But Keith told him that he didn't HAVE to become a Christian. His religion is a personal decision between him and God. So Salif stayed.

Keith witnessed to Salif often but he stuck by the doctrine he learned in the Koran. Keith would invite Salif to church and he said he would go like all nice Africans do with no intention of going. After two years of invitations Salif finally consented to go to church. While Keith preached Salif knew that the love of Christ was the real answer but he couldn't turn from Islam. Salif is Moray and speaks Moray so he didn't understand all the French. Especially the word Salvation. Keith described the French word for Salvation as a gift to be accepted and that God is offering us the gift of Christ to either accept or reject. After attending church for 3 Sundays he raised his hand at the invitation and accepted Christ. He said he was nervous as a Muslim to believe in Christ in front of so many people but he knew it would be worse to go to hell.

Salif has grown in the Lord for the last three years and memorized many verses. He followed Keith back to his home country of Burkina Faso and has been a huge help in starting ministry here in Ouagadougu. Salif translates all of Keith messages into Moray since many from Burkina don't speak French.

Ivory Coast

Tonight I had the opportunity to sit down at a coffee shop (a stand on the side of a wide dirt road full of large ruts with about five wobbly wooden tables scattered on the bare, brown ground) with Keith and three pastors from the Ivory Coast. It was dark without the aid of streetlights, which made it hard to see their faces. I could see their clothes but at night they are practically invisible except for their eyes and teeth. We had a great time talking about their ministries, the needs, and their future.

This is what I learned from Boli, Marselline, and Ambrous:

-The Ivory Coast, though having been labeled an "Evangelized Country" by the Southern Baptist Mission Board and many Independent Baptist missionaries is still in deep need and crisis. The recent war has left the northern part of the country empty of churches. During the war the pastors in the North prayed it would cease. The Northern rebels seeing this and obviously not wanting the war to stop threatened to kill them. Most pastors and all Independent Baptist pastors from the North left, their churches were looted, their land stolen, and now there are no churches. The Western part of Ivory Coast is in deplorable shape as well on the border of Liberia. The war in Liberia that recently ended caused many refugees to spill across the border and left chaos on the whole Western side. Lawlessness is rampant and missionaries have been afraid to go there. So there are only a couple Baptist churches amongst millions in Western Ivory Coast. I personally tend to like to block off the world so I don't need a burden for the "reached" parts. It's just my effort to lessen my burden and focus on my corner.

-They have all gone through poverty and worked hard in God's work. They have been soul winning and discipling all week with a great attitude while having left their churches back in the Ivory Coast. Marselline's church runs over 120 while the other two are running around 60 with very little finances. I think they can be commended for their work. The exciting thing is they will be. They'll be so far ahead in the proverbial "Jewel Receiving Line" in heaven from their American counterparts that.... well, I don't know how to express it except to say the last shall be first and the first shall be last. I will be humbled to follow them in line. They are some great men of God.

Sunday Report
I really enjoyed preaching in the two new churches of Ouagadougou, Burkina Faso this morning. Like all invited preachers I wanted to be a blessing but knew that the real work was done and will be done by Keith, his hard-working wife, and the new believers that make up those two churches.

The first church is on the edge of town and I mean edge. It is the end of the road. After leaving the pavement (which didn't last long) we weaved through 15 minutes of dirt road in a maze of mud huts. There were around twenty-five adults and over 100 kids. The kids stayed under the grass mat while the adults met in the small building with a tin roof. They sang in French and their native Moray. Keith bought five acres out in the boonies. The city is growing so fast as Africans from the surrounding countries are pouring in. Soon this area will be very strategic.

The second service was held inside the city. There were over sixty adults there. The most exciting thing about the morning was a young man named Soleman who came searching for God. He was a Muslim but praise God, Keith led him to the Lord this morning. That was very exciting and we are praising the Lord for that this afternoon.

I'll be heading back to see my beautiful wife up north tonight. I want to beg everyone who reads this to pray and plan for laborers for West Africa. I have never seen Muslims and Animists alike coming to Christ like this. We desperately need to train leaders amongst these people. The field is ripe here and God is moving and calling for laborers. I am asking God to allow my friend Tyler and I to raise up someone by this time next year to come to Burkina Faso. We'll show Islam in Africa the love of Christ from the north and the south.

October

Train Ride Home

I returned from Burkina Faso yesterday. After my flight I had a seven-hour train ride and got the chance to witness to four people. The train has compartments that hold a max of eight people. When I got on the train I was in a compartment with just one guy named Hassan. He was an older man with a full Islamic beard. Within five minutes of talking to him we were into the subject of "religion". As soon as he figured out that I speak Arabic (sort of) he assumed that I must be a Muslim. When I told him I wasn't, he asked, "Why not?" Great question. So I answered him. From Adam to Isaiah to Jesus, The Lamb of God. He sat and stared at me having never heard an educated response to his question before. After about fifteen minutes I asked, "What do you think about that?" His response was simple: "Your wrong." Thanks for the stimulating rebuttal Hassan! So as I was in the middle of witnessing to him three more people joined our cabin and were obviously fascinated by our conversation.

When Hassan's stop came he pulled a box of clove incense that Muslims use and gave it to me as a gift. Quite the opposite reaction I expected.

As soon as he left the conversation picked up again from the other three who had come in. It was Othman, his modern, no-head-cover wearing fiancé Hanan, and her head-cover wearing mother, Zohara. They were amazed to hear stories about prophets that they had never heard of. However, they concluded that if the Koran doesn't mention them then they must be false prophets. Those three rode all the way with me to my stop. All seven hours I was reasoning with these four Muslims from the Bible. It was great language practice. We didn't have a Koran but I had my Arabic and English Bible so we opened it and read from Isaiah, Genesis, John, etc. When we got off the train Othman promised to read the New Testament that I had given him as a gift. They were heading to my city to try and retrieve Zohara's youngest son who had ran away from home and was attempting to escape to Spain. I called him today and they had found him and taken him home. I told him my family had been praying for him.

94

The big difference between these Muslims of North Africa and the Muslims of black, sub-Sahara Africa is their passion. Those Muslims south of the Sahara are typically ignorant of the Koran and the Bible. They are Muslims much like South American's are Catholic. Since they can't read Arabic they don't have a clue what their prayers or memorized verses mean. The Arabs of North Africa know more and want to argue but they don't know as much as they think they do. I think the key is to get them reading the New Testament. The entrance of the Word brings light.

Unconventional Evangelism

The devil is winning the fight in the "closed" countries of the world where evangelism and church planting are illegal. Those two things, evangelism and church planting, are what we were commissioned to do by Christ. So while we are studying hard on the language we are also keeping our eyes and hearts open for unconventional ways of mass evangelism.

Here are a few things we are trying:

1. Email Evangelism- We have collected over 2,000 email addresses now. We are sending them emails telling a story from the life of Christ and offering a free New Testament. We have already received many requests from around the country.

2. Internet website- alnour.com and arabicbible.com are two websites run by Arabic Bible World Outreach with Michael Hajj. They are well known through out the Arab world. We receive daily requests from North Africa for Bible study lessons and Bibles.

3. Message of Hope- The Message of Hope Project is attempting to mail 20,000 letters to the homes of North African Muslims this year. Next year we want to triple that. 300 volunteers from the US and other countries are already stepping up to send these 90-cent letters. Our goal is to hit 1 million homes eventually. We are receiving requests from these letters.

4. Text Message- For $250 we can send 5,000 text messages to cell phones with 160 characters. Next month we hope to send a message to draw out those who may be interested more in learning about the Christ of the Bible. This is purely experimental. We'll try anything

once!

5. Skype us!- North Africans can call our Skype name anytime and talk to us live with questions about the Bible.

Beggars with Cell Phones

After my trip to West Africa God really worked on my heart for those from that region who are traveling through our country. There are thousands of central Africans who travel north trying to get to Europe. They end up stuck often on the route.

So after returning to our city my eyes were opened to that need that I hadn't done anything about before. So my first day back I met a guy named Jeffrey who is a black African (as opposed to an Arab) from Nigeria. First time I met him on Monday he told me that he has been here four years as an illegal and can't get a job. He spends his day begging on the streets to make money enough to live. So I saw him for the second time and he remembered my name as well as I did his. I was in my car without much time but told him I wanted to see him again. His response: "Why don't you take my cell phone number?" Sure. Why didn't I think of that? Take the cell phone number from the   beggar.

I called him yesterday and we met out on the street by his apartment. Right. He has an apartment. He explained to me about the hundreds of Africans from Nigeria, Ghana, Liberia, Senegal, and other countries that are stuck here illegally. This time he told me he was a Christian and that he meets with 50 other Nigerians in the woods on Sunday for a "church service". Don't know if it's true but he invited me to come and check it out so we'll see. So we prayed together on the street and I promised to see him again.

Today I met Miguel. Miguel is a black African from Equatorial Guinea, a Spanish Speaking Central African country. Miguel is here on a scholarship from a UN program along with 50 other Africans from his country. He is studying in the university but many of his compatriots don't have jobs or money. He is catholic and so are his friends. We are going to be witnessing to these guys and others.

Firsts

Today was full of some firsts:

96

First #1: We have over 200 names and addresses on a database that we have compiled. These 200 people all have two things in common. First, they all are Muslims. Second, they have all asked for Bibles. So over the last few months we have sent them New Testaments, the Bible on CD (Thanks to ABOM), and the first lesson of "All the Prophet's Have Spoken" (a Bible study course beginning with Adam). Some of them have responded with their phone numbers so today I called four of them. They were all happy to hear from us. One said that he had accepted Christ around one year ago. Another is 21 and lives about 5 hours from us. Another is a farmer who lives about 7 hours from us. Pray for these guys as they seek the truth.

First #2: A few days ago I met a West African guy named Jeffery. Having just returned from that area, the Lord has worked in my heart to witness to the Africans that are stuck here trying to get out. Jeffery is 28 years old and has been living here for 8 years. He, like many West Africans came through the Sahara desert on foot in hopes of paying off a boat captain to smuggle him into Europe. He told me that there were a lot of guys like him but I had no idea how many. My co-worker and I met tonight with him so we could witness to him. We met him in front of a closed coffee shop (it's Ramadan) and he took us to meet his friends. We walked uphill through winding roads in the poorer section of town picking up black Africans (that's how they refer to themselves) as we walked. By the time we stopped we ended up in an alley with over 20 Nigerian men.

We sat down and listened to their stories. They have been here from anywhere from one year to eight years. They are not allowed to work by law. They are not allowed to beg. They are not allowed to exist. One of them told me that he has been arrested three times and dragged to the border of the neighboring Muslim country where he was dropped off in the desert. Some have come with their wives. Three of them have a wife and kid or kids with them. Some of them have a small room they rent to live in. Some live in the woods under a tent. Some of them have attempted the cross into Europe a number of times and failed. They survive by begging for food and money. If you saw them you wouldn't guess they were beggars. Most of them came with quite a bit of money in their pockets that they had saved for years in order to make it into Europe. So they dress nice but have nothing to do all day. Some of them go to the Catholic church for expatriates and others gather for "fellowship" in the woods (That's what they told me.) Some of them claimed to be born again. They asked me if they are welcome in my church. I had to tell them that I don't have one that meets in English but maybe we'll be starting one. Before I left them we all bowed and prayed together on the street. Pray for them and the 600+ illegal West Africans they say live in this city.

First #3: I gave a whole Bible to a good friend I have been witnessing to. He has read a lot of the New Testament I have given him. Today I visited him and he recounted for me the stories in Genesis and Exodus that he has been reading. He laughed at how much of the Old Testament Mohammed stole and plagiarized in the Koran. He asked me tonight, "Tell me, what do I need to do to be a Christian?" He has asked me that before but I felt before that he was asking what "works" does he need to perform if he wants to be a Christian. Tonight I felt as if he really wants to be a follower of Christ. Since we didn't have much time, I told him to read Romans ten tonight and he can be a Christian by tomorrow after we talk about it. He was surprised by that response and excited. So we'll see tomorrow. Please pray for him as well.

Impatiently waiting

Tonight is "Laila el Qader". It is a BIG Muslim day. God is working in my heart to give me a deeper love and patience with the North African Muslims. I get quickly discouraged. We can only expect a harvest AFTER the planting and watering and, well, whatever else them farmer types do. So we are praying, planting, watering and only doing a fraction of what we need to do to get the Word out. Language is the key. I am preaching tonight in Arabic and then again on Sunday.

PLEASE pray for Pastor Austin Gardner and Missionary Chris Gardner. They are hosting and preaching at a large pastor's conference in Arequipa right now. I am begging God for a Latin pastor to surrender to come help us reach Muslims in North Africa.

I was chatting with Karim the law grad today. He is in school getting his masters degree. So as we chatted today he told me that he has read the whole New Testament. I asked him if he had accepted Christ yet and he responded: "I believed. I just want to learn more now." So we talked for an hour and he is really digging into the Word. Pray for him. I hope to visit him again this week or next. It is hard to disciple someone six hours away.

Slaves Made Free in Christ

I have really been enjoying yesterday and today a visit from one of my favorite people, Ahmed. He is a new believer from a mountain city who now lives close to the church we go to on Sundays. Five years ago he saw Joyce Meyers preaching on Satellite TV and wrote them to receive a free Bible, though he didn't believe what they were saying. Seriously, you caught that right, Joyce Meyers preaches in Arabic here in North Africa. Obviously it is a voice over. I haven't watched it but I imagine it is a female voice over.

So he started receiving correspondence from them. He later moved to the north about an hour from us where he was working in construction. Last year the national pastor of the church we attend received his address from Joyce Meyer's group and visited him. In May of this year he made the decision to believe in Christ. In June he started attending our church. He is obviously darker than the rest of the northerners here and talks different but he always has a smile and is eager to learn anything about the Word.

I pick him up on our way to church every Sunday. I have been asking him to come visit us and so yesterday he called me and told me that he had a few days off work and is in our city. So we have been together since yesterday talking about the Word non-stop. It's great.

Last night we had a Bible study with three other guys. One of them was Miguel from Equatorial Guinea. He spoke Spanish so Cesar translated while I taught the Bible study in Arabic. It was pretty crazy and didn't really work well, but we had a good time anyway.

He, as a brand new Christian, is fasting with everyone else for Ramadan. I asked him yesterday why and got a surprise: "Because I haven't been baptized yet." So I picked up on that and assumed he doesn't know the very basics about being a Christian. So from talking yesterday and today I have found out after having been a "Christian" since May that he thinks the Bible teaches that Baptism washes away sin.

99

So we have been working on that all day. We have finally got nailed down the purpose of baptism and the fact that if he has believed and called on Christ for salvation that he is already a Son of God. That blew him away. He had a huge smile on his face as we went from verse to verse explaining them. It was great.

Then I figured I had better attack the subject of the law AFTER believing in Christ. We saw in the Bible how we don't need to fast during Ramadan since we have freedom from those chains in Christ. So today he started with a drink of water. It was the first time he had ever drunk or eaten anything during Ramadan in his 30 years of life. Crazy. So he really pigged out after that and started eating everything in sight. It was hilarious.

He also got a notebook for his daily devotions that he has never done before. Altogether I have been stumbling through the Word with him in Arabic for about eight hours over the last two days. It has been a great and mind stretching time. We are praying and working now to witness to his family and friends.

Thinking Out Loud
I had the opportunity to preach in the North African church again today. It was a great privilege and very challenging. My mistakes were many. They were more than I have time to list but, nonetheless, a good opportunity to practice my language. I will be traveling this week to do some follow up on some contacts that have written our website.

Truth sinks in...eventually
Ahmed left today after being with us for three days and two nights. After I posted yesterday we all ate dinner at my house to talk again. Now remember, we had been talking about the purpose of Baptism ALL day. So I was real proud about all he had learned and how far he has come under the great teacher that I am. So I proudly prompted him to explain to Cesar WHY he was going to get baptized. To my horror he responded, "To repent from sin." NOOOOO! I wanted to catch the words and stuff them back in his mouth. So much for being a great Bible teacher.

It is amazing how long it can take for truth to sink in. But then I have to remember that he has been a Muslim for 30 years and just two months ago started attending our church. This is really the first time anyone has explained this stuff to him. So we went over it again. For about an hour we illustrated it with mock baptisms quoting Gal 2:20 and Rom 6. Then for another hour we talked about all the things that happened when he believed in Christ. He filled up two pages on that one.

So FINALLY he got it. He could quote the verses. Around 10 pm after asking him ten times why he was getting baptized he said, "So the water can wash my sins." He laughed his head off because he could see he scared me to death with that one. But he got it. Praise God (not the teacher).

Before he left this afternoon we went to the top of the hill that looks over the 1 million plus people. We read about what Christ feels for people and how he had compassion on them as sheep having no shepherd. He told me that he is going to go home and share all that he had learned with his brother and nephew who live with him. He said he hadn't told them much before because he didn't know what to say. He told them he is a Christian but didn't know how to explain any of it. Hopefully now he can.

Follow Up Trip Two

All last week I have been making phone calls, receiving phone calls, emails, letters (the old kind, you know, on paper) from people all over this country who are responding to our website asking for Bibles, Bible study, Jesus Film, etc. Monday night I just couldn't take it any longer so I called up Ahmed, and asked him if he wanted to go on a little trip to visit some of these "seekers". He, being on vacation from his job for almost two weeks for the end of Ramadan holidays, and always willing to catch a free ride around the country, readily obliged. I told him that I wanted to leave Tuesday early so he was to call me when he got in town. He lives an hour away.

So about 5:30 my cell phone wakes me up with Ahmed's voice on the other side. "I am here." He says. Wow. Little earlier than I expected but great. So we pack the wife and kids and Ahmed up in the car and head out of town on our three-day trip. I didn't know exactly where we were going. I had written down about ten names of people I wanted to visit but had three in particular who I wanted to hit. Anyone else would be a bonus.

About an hour out of town I realized I had forgotten our passports. Now, you can't stay in any hotel (at least any that I have checked into) without providing your passport or National ID card. So I knew at that point we'd have to trust God to supply us a place to sleep. The first city we ended up in is about 4.5 hours from us. It is a beautiful and very ancient city. It houses one of the oldest operating universities in the world. This city is known as being the center of Islamic studies for this country and all of North Africa. Most of the religious leaders are trained in this city. This city boasts more Mosques' per person than any other city in our country. They are very proud of their religion.

After grabbing a sandwich we coordinated a meet up with Ayoub. Ayoub is 19 and studying first year law. He had contacted our website a few weeks ago to ask for a whole Bible. I had talked to him on the phone last week and got the feeling he was pretty genuine. I dropped my wife and youngest kid off to shop in the old Medina while I and Ahmed and my oldest kid met Ayoub.

Waiting for these contacts, which I have done a few times now, is a funny experience. I sit there scanning everyone to see if they look like they may be "the person". Funny thing is everyone looks suspicious. When Ayoub showed up we were talking on our cell phones to each other. That made it easier.

So we did the traditional kiss on the cheeks I am not big on making the actually kissing noise. I prefer just to bump cheeks. I actually hit noses with a guy yesterday while we switched from cheek to cheek four times. Then we made our way to a coffee shop close by and all four grabbed a seat and some mint tea.

As we talked I learned that Ayoub has four siblings and was born and raised in that city. I asked him why he wanted to learn about the Bible. His response, "I want to know the truth." Good answer. Stupid question. He seemed to have a good grasp on what Jesus did and why he did it. I asked him if he had believed on Christ and he held his thumb and forefinger up close together and said, "Close".

About that time my precious son (I could strangle him sometimes) Starts yelling, "I gotta go pee pee. I gotta go pee pee." So I head off to the bathroom with my bursting son while Ahmed and Ayoub sit. Now Ahmed is not your typical Christian here. He has a boldness that few do. All his family knows that he is a Believer in Christ. Not a second after I left, Ayoub asked Ahmed if he believed on Christ and he responded in the affirmative. Ayoub then told Ahmed that he as well had believed in Christ.

Upon my return we went back to my car and sat in the air conditioning and read through some prophecies in Isaiah and then Rom 10 about exactly "How" to become a Christian. From there we picked up my wife and headed into the old Medina. This medina is more than 1000 years old. After only about a five-minute walk into the Medina Ayoub leads us into a house. It is a five-story house totally open in the middle surrounded by the windows of the rooms above. There were verses from the Koran posted all around with the audio of the Koran being methodically sung reverberating off the old plaster walls.

We sat down on their traditional seats and I thought the place was a tourist shop. I was waiting for the guy with a cigarette lighter to jump out and start showing us rugs. But to my surprise this was Ayoub's house! He took us through it and onto the roof where you could see the city and the surrounding mountains. He took us to his room where he kept his New Testament and French correspondence with a New Age Religious group called "Eckankar, The Ancient Science of Soul Travel ". I had no idea what that was till I just now googled   it.

When we arrived downstairs again we found Ayoub's mom had arrived and was insisting on speaking French to my wife. My wife knows only how to count to 10 in French. When I arrived she realized that my son and I have names of "prophets" in Islam They think all the prophets were Muslims so anybody with an Old Testament name must be a Muslim in their opinion. So she asked me if I was a Muslim. "No, I am a Christian. But I have read the Koran." I responded.

"So your a Muslim then." She reasoned.

"No. Still a Christian. I read the Koran and believe that Jesus died for our sin and rose from the dead."

"So you don't believe in the prophet?" She pushed speaking of Mohammed.

"Well, uh, no, no I don't. I believe only those who agree with the truth of the prophets and the Messiah in the Injeel."

"Oh. My son Ayoub reads the Injeel. But he is NOT a Christian!" She insisted raising her voice.

I could tell that it wasn't going to get a whole lot better so we politely made our exit. His mother said goodbye by assuring me that I would become a Muslim shortly. What are you supposed to say to that?

Ayoub is going to have a very difficult time following Christ with his surroundings, if in fact he will determine to. Please pray for him. I am not sure if he has made that committed decision to believe on Christ yet. He will need the courage just to think for himself.

After we left there we were off three more hours south to Ahmed's house where he was born and raised in a small village in the mountains. It was definitely the most rustic stay we have had yet. Mud walls. Temperatures around 40 degrees. No chairs or tables. Just blankets on the ground. My car was the only one in the town.

After our stay with Ahmed's family in their village we headed out to meet our second contact. After traveling for about two hours we met up with him at a park. We soon realized he didn't have much interest in the New Testament we sent him. He was more interested in a job in Europe. When he realized that I was not giving away European jobs he jetted. So we prayed for him and left.

Three hours later at about 7 pm we ended up on the coast for our third meeting. This guy showed up at a coffee shop off the main road. He has been studying the Bible for years searching for the truth. He has a wife and a son. The first thing he told us is that he believes in Jesus Christ but that his faith is small. The more we talked we realized that he is afraid to meet with the church, afraid to tell his wife, friends, or anybody about this Christ he has discovered. Ahmed started in on him, really rough. Telling him that he can't be a follower of Christ and be afraid. This guy has been afraid for years. I don't know if it's possible to change someone who has trained himself to be fearful instead of faithful.

After sixteen plus hours of driving in two days we arrived back home. We read many chapters in the Bible together in the car. Ahmed doesn't know it but we have gone over the first four lessons in the discipleship course: The Word of God, Salvation, Eternal Security, and Baptism. Ahmed has read his Bible now and kept a journal on it for nine straight days. We are headed toward one month and excited about it.

Phone Calls

Said wrote our website two months ago asking for a New Testament. After sending him a CD with the Bible on it and a first lesson he called me while Ahmed and I were traveling. Ahmed took the call. He had profusely thanked Ahmed for sending the material and asked for more. Last night I got a phone call from Said again. We talked for about fifteen minutes and he told me his story.

One year ago his six-month-old son fell sick. His family was out of town and he was an unemployed computer repair technician at that time. He needed around $100 or his son would not get the medical treatment he needed and he would die. Said didn't know what to do so he went out trying to sell things. In one hour he made $120 and was able to pay the doctor to give medicine to his son. At that point he realized that God had done a miracle and according to him began to get serious about searching for God.

Four months ago he found a Muslim book about the "Prophet" Jesus in a Suq in his home town (which happens to be about 14 hours driving distance from us). I don't know what the book said but it touched his heart. He found our website www.arabicbible.com and began to read the Bible. It was through that website he contacted us. He told me that he wants to be a Christian but needs to know more. So I prayed for him and hope that he is serious. It is extremely difficult for me to know exactly how to lead him over the phone. He is supposed to be reading the first chapter of John today. Tomorrow we will talk about it. Pray for him, his wife, and little boy. He lives in a city of over a million that has somewhere around 30 believers. If you know Khalid Intidam from Vision Baptist Church, it is where his parents are originally from in the South.

That was call number 1.

This afternoon I got a call from Ahmed. He had gone home after our trip. This was his ninth day reading the Word daily. Of course we said our two-minute hello that Arabs do: Good day. No problems? Family good? Kids good? No problems? God bless you. God help you. yadda yadda. Then he dropped the bomb: "So, have you read your Bible today?" Busted! I had stayed up late working last night and got up late this morning just in time to get to the office. So I didn't read my Bible and I had to admit it. Honesty is best. "I have read three chapters." He gloated. He was being a punk but I loved it.

That was call number 2.

God works on His end

Said called back today around 10 am. I had told him yesterday that he was supposed to read John 1 and call me back. I was in language school so I had to step in the other room to take his call. Our teacher is not a believer. I asked Said if he had read John 1. He said that he had but it had cost him quite a bit of money to print it all out off our website at the Internet cafe. I figured out that he had printed out the whole book of John and read it and not just the first chapter. Oh, well. No harm done.

So we started with the first verse and talked about how the Word was God and the Word was made flesh and dwelt among us. He read a verse and then we talked about it all the way down to verse 12 where we learned that to all those who believe on the name of Christ are given power to become sons of God. From there we went to Romans 10:9-10. I told him that all he has to do is confess Jesus as Lord and his death and resurrection. As I said it I noticed he was writing it down. "Now, what should I say?" he asked. I saw that I was confusing him by telling him that there is no magical sentence so I just told him, "Pray to God and say something like this, "Lord, I know I am a sinner. I thank you for sending Christ to die for my sins and be my Savior. I want to accept him and receive eternal life." He made me repeat it a few times as he wrote it down.

About 20 minutes later I got on Skype and this is it's translation:
S: Salam
A: Salam and grace from Jesus Christ
A: Have you accepted Christ yet?
S: Yes
A: When?
S: I believed in Jesus Christ
S: He saved me from my sins
A: Read Romans 10: 9-10
(He reads it)
A: So, when did you confess Jesus as Lord with your mouth?
S: Today
A: Amen!
A: Write down this date that you became a Christian today.
A: Does your wife know that you believed on Christ and that you read the Bible?
S: Yes. I am working to see her believe with me so she can be saved to.
A: Very good!
A: The Bible says in Mat. 10:32-33 that we must confess Christ before men and Christ will confess us before the Father. (I copied the verses)
S: That's right. That's the truth.
A: Amen.

So praise God. Only God could do something like that. It was exciting to see those literal hours spent memorizing John 1 in Classical Arabic pay off in such a huge way.

God will work on his end if we do our part to communicate the gospel to people on our end. He is the Savior of those who call, the Convictor of those who hear, and the Enabler of those who preach. Only He can receive the glory.

Irish and Africans
The world is smaller figuratively than it has ever been but I have found some of its corners in my last two trips.

My most recent trip was to visit Keith Shumaker in Burkina Faso, West Africa. One day out soul winning with two African brothers we were invited into the home of a Muslim family. Only the mom and her 5 small children were home. The smallest was crying her head off and running in fear hiding behind her mom and older siblings. I asked one of the African brothers what was her problem. They told me that she had never seen a white person and she was afraid I would eat her.

So now I am in Northern Ireland. I have never seen so many white people in all my life. I went to the grocery store with my friend Travis and that is all there is here: white people. No blacks, browns, yellows...just white. We have been door knocking now for three days. I have probably knocked a couple hundred doors and ALL white people. So, I was talking yesterday to David, a 40-year-old man attending Travis' church. David told me about a trip he had taken a few years ago when he was in his twenties to America. It was the first time he had EVER seen black people in person. He was in a room with twenty of them and he said he really was afraid they were going to kill him. He got over his fear and then observed in amazement their bi-colored hands (you know, black on one side, white on the other.)

So the African thought the white man would eat her and the white man thought the Africans would kill him. That's amazing in 2007. I am looking forward to getting back to the brown people.

November

Worst Case Scenario

If you remember from about two weeks ago I wrote about Said, a guy from a city in the south fourteen hours from us, who accepted Christ over the telephone. Well, he left his wife and son yesterday to come meet us. Now that's a huge trip. Fourteen hours just to meet someone you've talked to over the phone.

So, here is the big dilemma amongst missionaries in the Muslim world. No one has a problem that we witness to people or even give out Bibles to people we meet. The problem comes when someone responds, like Said. Many have told us that Said is either a secret policeman coming to sniff me out and kick us out of the country or he just wants money or a job in Europe and will probably black mail us to get it. Those are the fears that control the work here in North Africa. I don't know if he is one of those two things but the truth is I have never been very good at doubting people and holding them in suspicion. So, I am going to go meet him and try to believe that he really is what he says he is: A new believer in Christ.

So I am nervous. Partly because when people "warn" you it always somehow makes its way into your subconscious and partly because my language is lacking and I know he is just going to think I am a complete amateur not ready to be helping him learn about God. Anyway, pray for him and us. We are going to move ahead for the glory of God and see what happens.

My friend Travis liked this quote so we are applying it in this situation as well as all situations we face: "Some think that the worst case scenario is expulsion, imprisonment, or even death. We must believe, like that first church, that the worst case scenario is disobedience to our Lord Jesus Christ." They may kick us out but I'd rather stand before God a "kicked out" missionary than a "disobedient" one.

If our light is hid...

We met with Said today around 10 am. It was Cesar, Ahmed, and I. So we met him at the bus station, exchanged holy kisses (two on each cheek to be exact) and drove to a nearby Coffee House. I was nervous as we pulled up to the bus station to meet him. As soon as I saw him I knew he was just a normal guy. He is very unassuming and has a look of sincerity that would rival Mother Theresa.

We sat and had coffee and eggs as we got to know each other. We all shared our testimonies starting with me. Ahmed stumbled a little expressing himself and didn't use all the spiritual language that we old-timers in the faith used but he didn't have the least hint of fear. Sure, he may not have polished his testimony to get support at some superficial missions conference but he connected with Said and that's what counts in the real world.

We went through John all again like we had over the phone. He said he has already believed on Christ and is bringing his wife along. He has not told his parents yet. One thing that impacted me that he said was that he has been looking for a church in his city for the last four months but can't find one. He said it in a real desperate way. He was so desperate to find the answers that he spent $50 for an overnight bus ride to see someone in the flesh who could explain more to him. He had never seen a Bible before today. I had the privilege of giving him one that was provided to us by BEAMS Bibles and smuggled in this summer. Felt like I was giving the man a million bucks.

If you want to find a church in the free world just look them up in the phone book or stop by the eight churches you pass on your ten-minute drive to work in the morning. If a Muslim living in a Muslim country wants to find answers in a church they have no idea where to look. There is no church listed in the phone book. No signs. No 1-800-prayer hotline. There are three house churches (maybe about 50 people in total) in Said's city of one million. But he can't find them. How many Muslims are in the darkness of their cities looking for light but have no idea where to find it? That is haunting. I thought that light always overcomes darkness? And then I realize, unless it's covered up. Is your light hid to those who are lost?

Paul, Tim, Faithful Men, and Others

There was a time when someone taught me how to read my Bible on a daily basis. I am a bum and I'll admit it but it wasn't until I was in Bible College. I had heard that I should read my Bible daily my whole life but never really got the habit down (because I am a bum)

110

until Austin Gardner showed my how to write it down ever day and have a partner that kept me accountable. So Ahmed who is a new believer since just May of this year is starting to do the same thing. About three weeks ago I taught him how to and he hasn't missed. He is through John and halfway through Acts. He wants me to read everything he writes. Great help for my Arabic but time consuming. He writes about half a page for each chapter. It's like his own commentary.

So Said's first question, who we met for the first time today, was "How do I read the Bible?" Since Ahmed was there he spent the next thirty minutes or so walking him through his devotional journal sharing with Said how to do it. It was great. Ahmed is not as bad as me. I usually act as if it was my idea but Ahmed kept telling Said over and over, "He taught me to do this." I want to encourage you to share with someone who doesn't know how to walk with God daily if in fact you do. Someday they'll teach someone else or maybe hundreds of others. Then those hundreds will teach thousands of others.

No difference...hmmm?

Had a great day today. The church we are going to baptized five men this morning. We were excited about being a part of it. It made me dream about the future. We met at 8:30 am before there would be anyone at the beach and baptized in the ocean. It was cold but good. There were a few fishermen within ear and eye shot but they barely noticed us. We pray, sang, yelled amen and everything.

Last night around 11 pm Ahmed and I were witnessing to the dude who watches the parked cars at night. Everyone pays him about $12 to walk around with a stick all night and protect our vehicles. So starting off the whole thing I mentioned to him how special Jesus is and how he needs to get to know him. He of course said that the Koran says, "There is no difference in the prophets." No let me think about that…

If only one "prophet" was born of a virgin...
If only one "prophet" was called the Messiah, the Promised One...
If only one "prophet" was called The Word Of God...
If only one "prophet" was present at creation...

Of which all of those things the Koran admits...would you say there is NO difference in him and the rest of those guys?

Hmm?

So, I told him that and he kept quoting the Koranic verse. We'll see if we can keep working on him.

Are you someone's hero, fool, or excuse?

Said just left on a bus for the 16-hour ride back to his city. He was with us for three days. We taught the Bible crash course to him from Genesis to Isaiah to John to Revelation. He really enjoyed it and we enjoyed him, no doubt. He has not yet told his wife that he is a believer in Christ. I challenged him before he left to do that ASAP. A guy was just baptized yesterday who believed on Christ eighteen years ago and his wife doesn't yet know! He told his son who is sixteen and now a believer. His son was baptized with him. His wife didn't even know they were being baptized yesterday. Every Sunday he tells his wife that he is going to work (he owns video game stores) and that he is taking his son with him. Can you imagine being that afraid of your wife!?

I have been thinking more about Said. What would it have been like if I was afraid of him burning us? Well, I thought about it this way: If he had been sincere in wanting to know about Christ and salvation (and I think he is) then I'd have been his **hero** for telling him about it. If he had been fooling me for money or if he were a police officer then I'd have been his **fool**.

One thing is for sure: if we fear men and not God we become everybody's **excuse** for why they didn't accept Christ. "I never heard!" they'll cry just before they are cast into the lake of Fire. "He didn't tell me!" Now they'll still go to hell because without Christ, there is no excuse good enough. But the blood will be on our hands.

Well, I'd rather be a **hero** for sure. I have been an excuse too many times and I don't like it. But I'll risk being a **fool** just so I can't be anyone's **excuse**. I have watched men of God like my pastor, Roger Green and just a few other great men of God (there aren't very many of them). They seem to be used and abused a lot. People consider them **fools** because they stick their necks out for people who burn them. People who are using them. People who aren't sincere. People like Judas Iscariot. He thought that Christ was his **fool**. In becoming a **"fool"** Christ bore our shame and became everyone's **hero** and no one's **excuse**. No one can point a finger at God and accuse him of not loving them. So I conclude that to be someone's **hero** you have to be willing to be his or her **fool**. Over and over again.

I wonder if you are someone's **hero, fool, or excuse?**

The Berbers

While Said was here we got the chance to talk about something that I have never fully understood but have always wanted to: the tribes that were here in our country before the Arabs came. In case you are as ignorant as I was about it, North Africa is NOT Arab predominantly. They speak Arabic as the national language but only around 30% of the population is Arab. That means that more than 24 million people in our country are not Arab. In 700 a.d. led by Idris, the Arab Muslim and first king, the Arabs ransacked all of North Africa and forced conversion to Islam by the sword.

That history is 1,300 years in the past and most natives are unaware that they have not always been Muslim. There was a very significant population of Jews and other religions including a weakened institutionalized form of Christianity by 700 ad. Many have called North Africa the Land of the Vanished Church since no trace is left of a strong church that once was here during and shortly after the time of the Apostles.

Anyway, so everyone in our country that is not Arab we call Berbers. But they don't call themselves Berber. The word Berber was used by the Roman Empire before Christ to refer to anyone under their control who was not a Roman citizen. So, since all of North Africa was under their control they called them Berbers. That name still is the popular name they are known by with foreigners. They don't necessarily get offended by it but they know you are completely ignorant of who they are if you call them Berbers.

Grouping them

So, everyone kind of looks alike to me, so how do I tell them apart? Well there are basically 2 groups of native people who pre-date the Arabs.

First, those in the south in the Sahara desert are called the Saharawis. Second are those in the northern half called the Amazighan. These have brown skin and are hard to tell apart from Arabs. These are also those commonly known as the Berbers and historically make up the fabric of the culture, government, and economy. These Amazighan are split into three groups: The Rifi in the Rif Mountains, the Zayen in the High Atlas mountains (that's where Ahmed is from), and the Shluh in the south (that's what Said is). The Shluh in the south are famous for being excellent merchants. They light up when you talk about buying and selling or a new business plan. If you want to know if someone is Shluh, just try that. The Arabs are spread out all over though they set up camp in just a couple cities when they arrived 1,300 years ago.

Their languages: The name for the grouping of their languages into one category is Tamazight. The Rif speak Tarifit, the Zayen speak Tamazit, and the Shluh speak Shilha. Said explained all this to me. From the time a child is born until the time he goes to school at the age of 5 that is the only language he knows how to speak because his parents use it in the home. He or she may know some Arabic but not well. In school they do all their reading and writing in Arabic and some French. Very few people read and write the native languages though an alphabet has been developed and is being implemented in some of the schools. You can see how this is important for the gospel!

From a young age a child knows he is not Arab. They know that the Arabs are not natural here because of the language. Many of the older people that never went to school only speak their native language. Ahmed's parents who are in their 70's understand some Arabic but only speak Tamazit. So there are many people we'll never reach in Arabic here. That is something we have lost in America is our heritage. I think I am part Hungarian and part English but really I don't have a clue. I am just American and my culture dates back a couple hundred years. So, those "Berbers" are more open to the gospel when they understand that Islam is a foreign religion as well as their Arabic language. For instance, check out this email we received from a reader in Rabat:

"Salam u alakum, I am from North Africa I am not an Arab, I am an Amazigh. I left Islam almost 4 years ago, but I did not convert to any other religion. I know a little bit about Christianity, I love Jesus Christ, but am actually not yet a Christian. Thanks for sending a copy of the holy book, I need to read it. Also, do you send books that explain the holy book in Arabic ? God Bless You all, Amen."

So we live in the north. The area surrounding us is traditionally an Arab area. There are however Amazighan who have moved up here for work. We have a huge burden to reach all these groups of people with the gospel. The Jesus Film has already been translated into their specific languages along with a few other resources.

Letter from

Said., who left last week, left this letter for us. It is a thank you to everyone connected with us and especially arabicbible.com. It is also a revealing window into the culture here in North Africa:

"In the name of God and Jesus Christ I write to you this letter,

First, I would like to thank you for the generous hosting and hospitality (toward me) and thank you for the Holy Bible, it is the most precious gift that I ever received in my whole life and I hope (desirous hope) to find myself in this book which is precious to my heart, and I hope that this book will greatly open my heart to the "believing" faith.

I am so happy that I got to be acquainted with you - and now that I am today among you - I will never forget Haroun, Kaisar and his wife, and likewise Ahmed, who is a son of my own country (my country man) - I will never forget you. I love you all from my whole heart because you are all good and I hope that God will extend His hand of help to you so you can do (Charity) good works and I will pray for that. I am so happy with the Christian faith and I deeply believe in Jesus Christ and that He suffered for us because of our sins. I thank God for this spiritual guidance that entered my heart and I will utterly strive to learn as much as I can and I will always pray for all - this is a promise from me to you and I will strive for God and Jesus Christ because He is worthy of all sacrifice.

Lord, I beseech you that you help Haroun, Kaisar, and Ahmed in doing what is good (Charity) and I like to thank because you are the cause for me to meet with them and I ask you that you bless them for all what they are doing as far as charity work for Jesus Christ and for you oh God

Lastly, I ask you that you always remember me in your prayers and for the whole world. May the God prosper you and may He bestow all goods to this nation . Thank you My greetings to you. Ahmed."

Lady Ramblings
From Jillian's Personal Journal

Jan 6

We have been so busy packing and saying our good byes I have got my priorities out of line. Lord, please forgive me for not putting you first in my life. I really can tell you have given me many victories. But Lord I can also see how the verse is true in Gal 6 about if you think yourself to be something when you are nothing you deceive yourself. I became confident in myself and I did not give you the credit. I am sorry for beginning to worry today. Lord, strengthen my walk with you. Help me overcome the negative thoughts and fears. Humble me Lord. Teach me to do your will. I want to serve you because I love you not because I am afraid. Guide me, Lord. I desire what you want for me.

Jan 7

Many times today my fears and doubts have been thrown up in my face. People saying things about Muslims wanting to kill Christians, terrorist attacks, etc. Also I have dealt with some crying parents. The Lord has been faithful. He calmed my fears and guided me through. I would pause and get the worried sick feeling in my stomach…and then God would take over. He would cause me to remember the tricks of the devil and how he doesn't want me to be thinking about him. Praise the Lord for helping me overcome today. I know no matter what happens, God is in control. Though my hand shakes to write it, I know he loves me and my family. He is in control. Whatever bad comes our way had to be ok-ed by our Almighty God and he knows best. Praise the Lord. I liked John 9:33 today. It reminds me of who I am and how I can do nothing without God. Jesus Christ is God.

Jan 8

I took a few minutes to read some of my thoughts from about six months ago. I can really see how the Lord has given me victory and helped me overcome some sins in my life. My thought life; anxiety, fear, worry in particular is the area I have the most sin. I used to sit and worry and stress literally all day long. I was a nervous wreck. I struggled with my salvation I was scared of dying and with time God showed me:

He loves me. He saved me when I asked him to. He cannot lie. He wants to use us for his glory. The worst-case scenario is we die and go to be with our Savior. Scary things are going to happen. I will not despair. God is in control. He always will be. For me to live is Christ and to die is gain. For many in the world they cannot say that. Empower me, Lord, as we leave to live among those who have never heard. Eph 1 is so awesome that we have Jesus Christ as our personal Savior. In whom we have redemption through his blood, the forgiveness of sin according to the riches of his grace!

Jan 9

Wow! I really believe Satan is trying to get me off course this week. My fears are all creeping back up. Lord, please forgive me for dwelling on my negative thoughts. Lord, please help me focus on you. Eph 2:14

Jan 13

My devotions have been so lacking these past two weeks. We have been everywhere saying our "goodbyes". I know the Lord is not pleased with my luke-warmness . I think in some ways it is spiritual warfare. Unfortunately I have not followed the Lord the way I know to. I have been in a bad mood and I have had a very bad attitude. Let me take a few minutes to regroup in my mind and ask forgiveness.

Lord, I need you, forgive me for relying on my own strength. Forgive me for my lack of love for your Word. Forgive me for not taking what you did for me on the cross seriously. Forgive me for taking your love for granted. I am truly sorry, Lord. I love you, Lord.

Jan 18

It has been a while since I wrote last but I have been reading the book of Philippians. It is a huge help right now. I have been a little shaky since we got here in North Africa a few days ago. I have many first impressions I would love to write down when I have some more time. It is late and we have a busy Friday planned. Everything is going pretty good. I realize now I need God so much more. I am excited to get to know my Savior more intimately.

Jan 19

I have a little time with both children sleeping to begin writing down all my first impressions of North Africa and a little about Spain. Well, first it is WAY different from anywhere I have been before. My first two days I spent paranoid and literally shaking. We are staying with an American family who are very, very cautious. I think this many have made me a little more paranoid. I felt scared all the time. So my first feeling: scared. Scared the people hated me. Scared they were going to kick us out. Scared they wanted to kill me because I am American. After three days, I don feel like that anymore!

My second impression of the people: over half of the women wear head coverings, many wear Djellabas. Women are very into style, beauty is very important. Women are very quite, rarely walking alone but more commonly in pares or accompanied by their husband. Maybe I am wanted to see this so I don't have to go out alone. There are far more men on the street than women. Lots of stares from men. Comments in Arabic soon I'll know what they are saying. The people keep to themselves. Smiles in the stores but not so much on the streets. Also, a woman staring is common.

I feel like a big time outsider. I went out today to buy a djellaba and new shoes so I can feel as if I fit in more. I try not to look at men. You don't have to worry about forward women because there doesn't appear to be too many women approaching men. I think I will be staying in my home more. With two kids it will be quite hard to get in and out of everywhere.

Third impression of the stores and markets. Very nice. It is way more modern than Arequipa, Peru. Lots of frozen and packaged things. Olives and citrus fruits everywhere. Yummy smelling spices. Enjoyable.

Jan 20

We are staying with a family so between them and the two children it is a bit hard to find time to sit and write a lot. Tonight I have to go to bed shortly but I wanted to write just a little. It is going to take some major getting used to here. I hate it that the women will not smile. Men stare and make comments, lick their lips, raise their eyebrows, etc. Tonight, surprisingly, even when we were out as a family. I dress extremely modestly here. I always have some type of long shirt. Overall I can really feel God at work in my life and in my heart. My fear and paranoia is dying down a bit. I have to have some courage and faith. I can't live here afraid all the time. Praise the Lord for his amazing grace and never ending love.

I have been reading Phil. The 4th chapter is a huge help to me right now. Be anxious for nothing! Rejoice in the Lord always!

Jan 21

We went to our first International Church meeting this morning and tonight we have "church" just my husband and I. What an experience.

Jan 22

Today has been not the greatest day so far. It is cold and rainy. I woke up struggling with my attitude. It is going to be hard to get around here without a car. We went out today to buy a coat and it was very difficult with both children. When we returned back the lady we are staying with informed me that people are getting in her words, "gun shy" of answering all our questions. We have always learned by asking questions. I guess we have been intrusive. I feel very lonely now. Like I don not have any friends here. Like they have each other, they know what going on and we are alone. I know that right now I need to take these things to the Lord.

Also, today I saw some scary things on the news. It is like one minute I feel bold and confident, trusting the Lord and the next minute I am terrified. I never had any feelings even close to this in Peru. The men are protective of their wives here so when you go to the market or grocery store you may see 50 people and out of the entire group you may see four or five women shopping alone. They are usually accompanied by their husband, friends, or other family. A young woman alone is a prime target for the men. The women also stare. Anyway, I have many negative thoughts going through my mind right now I want to take some time to ask forgiveness for them and to regain my focus.

The Bible says be careful for nothing. God does not want me to be worried and full of concern. When I am worried and troubled I am sinning, Also, in chapter 2 it talks about how we appear weak to the enemy when we are afraid. I am a believer in Jesus Christ. The Son of God, Almighty Creator of everything, Jesus Christ who died on the cross for me for my sin. Jesus Christ who is coming again. I have victory IN JESUS. I want everyday to grow closer to Him! This is not an easy place to live or do ministry. I pray that He will use me to be a light in this dark world.

A side thought, something I have to write down: I know when we move into a new culture we are not supposed to say we hate things but I do here. I hate how women will not smile in public. It is sad. Maybe one out of seventy will give a half smile. On the street I cannot even make eye contact of any kind with a man. This is considered forward. And a stare in the direction of a man is come on, according to a book I read about the culture. I don't think I will ever fit in here. I know I will be in my house a lot more. Every home and apartment has a terrace so the women who are not allowed out can get some fresh air. I was sitting at a restaurant today with my husband and the kids and for five minutes I counted the people walking by. It was 17 to 1 male female ratio. And the one female was with her husband.

Jan 23

Yesterday was a very difficult day for me. Mainly I guess because it was my first time with a complete feeling of loneliness. The people we are staying with think we are being nosey and intrusive. I don't know what to think about that. They have a club and we don't belong. We are not members. This is something I am really not used to. It is weird because they are so nice and hospitable. I guess we just need to focus on getting a house and keep to ourselves more. That is not going to be easy for us to do.

I am sick this morning, my nose is pouring and I didn't go to bed until around 3 am. I couldn't sleep. I am not sure about all the "security measures". I pray that God will change my heart and let me see the good.

I am still reading Philippians. Today in chapter four I noticed a verse that I really need to keep in mind: vs 11. Not that I speak in respect of want: "for I have learned in whatsoever state I am, therewith to be content." I have had a bad attitude about not having a clothes dryer.

121

Little things I really need to get right with God about. He is so good to us. Prayerfully we will be signing on an apartment tomorrow. Praise the Lord!

Jan 24

Today was a little boring, I was sick with a temp all day. I stayed inside with the children. I talked with Shayma on the phone so that was great. She is still hanging out with people who take her to church so that it good. We have just signed for our apartment so probably tomorrow we will be sleeping in our new home. A verse that really sticks out today in my Bible reading is Proverbs 24:10 "If thou faint in the day of adversity thy strength is small." Beth Dixon, a friend from GA sent me an encouraging email with a verse from Is. 49 reminding me that my strength is in Him. He has me in his hands.

Jan 25

Today we moved into our new home. It is very late and I still haven't spent my time with the Lord. I am going to read a few chapters and go to bed. Tomorrow I hope to write more. God is good. I am going to bed with an excitement about being here. Little by little we are going to feel at home! Praise the Lord!

Sunday, Jan 28

Today we went to the International church again. It is so many different groups combined. Different languages, cultures, and ages. Maybe even beliefs. It is a blessing to meet together and worship God. Even if it is only once a month. At least we can sing to the Lord and have fellowship. It is also good for the children.

I just had a very busy night cooking, shopping for food, cleaning, and washing. Also cleaning the veggies. Time consuming. We had two students over to eat. I am cooking camping style right now. It is kind of fun I guess. I just pray our container gets here okay. I am tired and I have yet to read the Word. I spent my quite time today studying Arabic. It is not going to be easy. I want God to give me a stronger desire to learn.

Monday, Jan 29

I am still struggling with the bad attitude I have had the past few days. I know it is sin and it is ugly. I pray that God will forgive me and help me to move forward. I need to be content in whatsoever state I am. After reading Galatians, I am reminded to walk in the Spirit. I have been giving in to the flesh so I need to ask forgiveness and walk after God. Following his Holy Spirit.

Tuesday, Jan 30

Today I woke up this morning and told God and my husband that I would have a better attitude. With God's help or should I say because of God. Today was a positive good attitude day. An extremely busy day. It is crazy. I stayed inside my house all day doing housework and I am perfectly fine with that.

February

Thursday, Feb 1

We are starting language school today so with the Lord's grace I am going to begin a new more disciplined day. We have been busy setting up in our house. We are now waiting for our container to arrive. It should be here within the next week. We will see. Things are getting easier as far as the culture. I am getting a little more used to things. I do stay at home a lot. Hopefully this will change, as we need to spend more time in the community learning the language. For right now at least, I am super busy in the house. Hopefully I will be able to train my helper, Fatima to do some of the housework. This would free up my time to do my language study and spend time with the kids.

Gal 5-6 My life verse Gal 6:9 was particularly encouraging this morning as we begin language school: "And let us not be weary in well doing: for in due season we shall reap if we faint not"

September

From Jillian's Blog Lady Ramblings
www.ladyramblings.blogspot.com

A little History...

Today we went to our church which is an hour and half away. It was a great service! I noticed that when it got time to go the people started acting a little sad. It is Ramadan here now. Easily the hardest time of the year for ex-Muslim Christians.

I sat with my friend Hayet she was sitting quietly by herself. I thought...."okay make yourself get over there and speak to her." So I sat with her and talked with her about her testimony. She has been a believer for ten years. Until one year ago she did not even know other Christians existed here. She told me it was a kind of alone no one could understand. But she said that smiling. She is a courageous woman. Her mother knows she not a Muslim. She talks about her faith with her family from time to time.

After I have one of those conversations I am always convicted of the lack of contentment I have in my life. I am always finding things not to like in my life. I find myself dwelling on the struggles of living here in this Muslim country. But this NOT where my only friends and family are. I have friends who I can share my relationship with God with, my friends that share the same desires and vision. Friends I can call and pray with. Friends that I praise the Lord for. But until last year Hayet knew of no one. And now she only knows five Christian women. I know God has us here for many reasons, one of which I truly believe is to be a friend to the believers. To provide the vital companionship that will help each other develop a closer relationship with God. I am blessed to know Hayet. She is an awesome person. I thank God that he is merciful with an undeserving person like me.

Eating in North Africa

I was thinking since the food here is really amazing I would share a few things with you from time to time! Living in any culture different from your own means changing what you eat. Fitting into any other culture means learning to cook the food they eat. Praise God the food here is amazing. Sometimes really different, but I haven't eaten anything gross yet! If you are trying to diet this is not the place to come!

Let me start by explaining HOW we eat here. No forks or knives needed. We eat from one huge plate/bowl in the center of the table. Here you eat the food with bread. Just scoop it up. It is a little messy but to them it is no big deal if you get food on the table or anything- it is normal. So, I actually think it is pretty fun. I try to make food from here every other day. Then I have our close friends taste test it. One is really honest, if you know what I mean!!

So here is a recipe for a common dish: Lamb Tajine (you could use beef)

2lbs lamb or beef
1 Large chopped red onion
2-4 cloves of Garlic
1/2 tsp saffron colorant
1/2 tsp ginger
2 tbsp chopped fresh parsley
1 tbsp chopped fresh cilantro
1 cube beef bouillon
1/2 tsp cinnamon
1/2 tsp cumin
1/2 tsp black pepper
1 tsp salt
1/4 C olive oil

-Sauté all the above ingredients in the oil until the onion is tender. Add 2 Cups of water and simmer just until the meat is tender -but NOT mushy. (Or you can put everything in a pressure cooker.) Add a variety of vegetables listed below. With the veggies add 2 grated tomatoes (just grate the whole thing, the peeling will separate.) 1/2 hour before the meat is finished.

Suggested veggies:
Green beans (not canned) peas, carrots, cauliflower. For an extra good Tajine fry the cauliflower with an egg before adding it.

Depending on the quantity of vegetables this serves 6-8 people. It is great the second day too!

I hope that is understandable Learning to cook in another language is always a challenge.

STUFFED!!!!

I had a really fun day today! This morning I just got some things done around the house. Nothing too exciting there. The normal breaking up toddler fights and cleaning up spilled juice on the floor. At around 2:00pm after a super quick lunch before the babysitter came (we don't like to eat in front of her during Ramadan) I went out with my friend who lives here in our building.

Most women don't like to go out unless they have to during Ramadan. They believe it is wrong to wear makeup during Ramadan. So they wait until after the sunset to get all painted up. But there are a few days of the month that every woman can eat and go about as normal. So we went out to buy some material to make new djellabas. Djellabas are the long robe like dresses that are very popular and stylish here. I really enjoy wearing them too. We had a great time. We bought some nice fabric and talked about designs for how to make them. Of all the women I saw out today I was one of 5 without the head covering. Everybody is very conservative during Ramadan. I am more obviously "the foreigner" than usual.

After buying our material we drove to a small town outside of our city to buy bread and fresh mint from the mountain women who ride there their donkeys in to sell their goods. It seems so crazy to have two drastically different cultures living so close together. In the city people live similar to people in any big city. But in the mountains here the women wear pointy straw hats with a bath towel stuffed up under it. That is really in style! It is literally a bath towel. Flowered seems to be the "in" thing.)

When we got back home my friend insisted that I get the kids and come to her house to eat the meal to break the fast for the day. So we went. I learned a lesson the hard way: Don't go eat dinner with people that haven't eaten all day if you have! I am so stuffed right now. Here the main dish every night is Harira. A really thick soup with meat, noodles, rice, beans, and vegetables. I had to eat the never-ending bowl of soup. I tried to share mine with the kids. That has worked for me in other countries. They just brought out more bowls and poured more soup! They will be up until one or two in the morning eating and watching TV. Then they wake up around 4 am to pray and eat again.

To end the night, my friend Miriam called me. She is working hard to convert me. She has set me up before. She told me to meet her somewhere and then had her friend who speaks English meet us to really get her points across. She is so passionate about Islam. I am just waiting until I can really speak Arabic well enough to get my points across.

An afternoon and evening of intense language and culture learning. I pray that God will use me in the lives of my friends here. This is the first time in my Christian life I have had actual friends that are lost and on there way to hell. Sure we enjoy each other's friendship and time, but we are so different. I think about that every morning when I wake up. Just how different we are. God has put me here to be a light to them. I love them. I pray that God will do the work only he can.

What not to wear...

"What to wear today?" A common question of women around the world. Well, I thought I would share this with you guys, so you can know a little bit about how we dress over here.

Here are some of my first impressions on the way the women dress here. Why is that important? Let me explain my impressions first then I will explain from my point of view.

When we came here it was cold so I will start there...
-I saw no skin except for the hands and the face of the women.
-Turtle necks, scarves, or head covering are a must.
-I felt naked if my neck was showing even a little bit!
-No ankles showing. If they wore long skirts they put tall boots or pants under their skirts.
-Very, very dressy clothes...0r super dumpy clothes (like pj pants under skirts with hot pink socks etc.)

-Everybody tries to match everything, even the frumpy girls who wear their pj pants try to match their pink cheetah print pj pants to their pink head covering.
-They either care a lot about what they look like (the majority) or they really don't care at all.

And as it got warmer...

-Everyday it seemed like the women would get a little braver
-Soon everyone was dressing more "normal"
-Still long skirts and long sleeve shirts
-If they wear pants their shirts almost always cover their bottoms completely
-Finally sandals of all kinds!
-Even in the heat they wear a lot of layers

So for me, I have spent this summer in long sleeves and ankle length skirts!! I have some friends who even follow that "dress code" when they go swimming in the ocean. For me, I just choose not to go swimming. Sitting on the beach in longs sleeves in 95-degree weather! Yeah!

I try to dress like them except for the head covering. If I wore a head covering everyone would assume I have become a Muslim. It is very important to fit in with the women around you. But it is also very important to establish a distinct difference. I don't want to be immodest by their standards. Although I do get told by some of my friends that I need to cover up my hair. I do darken my hair to draw less attention to myself. It is obvious when I dress like them they feel honored and pleased that I want to be like them. One of my friends got really disappointed when I told her I wasn't going to wear my djellabas in America. I will always be an outsider to them because so much of their culture is centered on Islam. Anything I can do to get me one step closer to them is something I am willing to do! I wish they could understand the freedom we have in CHRIST.

Hospital vs. Clinic

Well, we got a first hand experience of the medical system at a private clinic our third week here. We spent three days in there with our daughter. She had roto-virus! YUCK!!! She had been sick for several days and she could not keep anything down. She was already very small so when she didn't seem to make any progress we knew she needed IV fluid. Since we don't have that at home we knew we had to go to the closest clinic only two blocks from us.

The room at the clinic was very nice. It even had its own refrigerator. It was a big room with a bed and a couch but I had to ask them to bring me a baby bed. I guess they thought a baby would be fine on a very tall hospital type bed with no railing. I had to pretty much stay on top of them telling them what to do. After two days they told us that our bill was getting expensive and we should go. Not "okay she is much better now" or anything like that. I had to tell them I wanted her to stay until we were sure she could eat and not just puke it all right back up! After three days she got better and we went home. So in this instance all I can say was the clinic served its purpose. Impressed I was not, but happy to return home with a healthy little girl!

The Hospitals are public and cheaper (sometimes FREE) and the care is not as good (of course this is what I have heard.) As far a need for health care here, it exists but the government is very strict on outside health care. I don't know all the details, we have just heard from several people it is very difficult for healthcare professionals to work here. The Muslim government knows that medical aid is often a tool of Christian missionaries.

Desert Anyone?

Here in North Africa we get some of the best citrus fruits in the world!! I love driving along the coast and seeing all the citrus and olive trees. It is really beautiful! Here is a recipe that is not really only North African but it is really easy and really good. My friend's family makes it all the time.

LEMON MOUSSE
1 can of evaporated milk
6 tbspoons of powdered sugar
The juice of a large juicy LEMON
-Chill the can of milk in the fridge an hour or so.
-Once the milk is chilled pour it into a large bowl.
-Add sugar, one spoon at a time stirring continually
-Whisk until the mixture becomes several times the volume
-Mix in LEMON juice. The mixture will thicken immediately.

-Freeze overnight...you can taste it now!

I love to eat this as a topping for raspberry or strawberry sorbet. It is good by itself too!
So there you have it, a super yummy and super easy little dessert.

No plucking

Eyebrows that is. I am never going to understand all the "rules" Muslim women are suppose to abide by, but come on. What is so spiritual about a uni-brow? My friend told me she really needed to go get her eyebrows waxed, but she said it was a problem during Ramadan. She said God doesn't like it when women pluck their eyebrows. When I asked "why" she kind of shrugged her shoulders and said, "He just doesn't like it and if we pluck our eyebrows when we get to Heaven God is going to rip out every little hair!" OUCH! But I guess this is pain she is willing to face or should I say a "rule" she is willing to break.

After a little study I understand a little bit about where this idea comes from: The idea from the Koran is that we should not change God's creation. -I guess for some it would be a big change. It even goes as far as to say that if the woman's husband asks her to pluck or shave she should refuse. I am all for being happy with how God made you, don't get me wrong. God did create us the way He wants us. But come on. I wonder how they feel about nose hair. Just an honest question!

I am learning more and more about the liberty we have in Christ! The TRUTH really does make you FREE. Even free to pluck your own eyebrows!

Nothing like Northern Hospitality!

Living here is teaching me so much! Muslim women believe one way to ensure their welcome into Heaven is by being hospitable! They really do an amazing job. So you can imagine the pressure I feel when we invite friends over. When they leave I feel like I have run a Marathon. Or should I say done an exercises DVD because I really don't know what running a Marathon feels like. Before I go on let me mention something very important:

If an Arab invites you to their home, they really mean they want you to come to their house. Excuse this next comment if you are the rare American who invites and really wants to always have people you barely know in your home.

You know how we are, we always say, "if you are ever in the area please, please come to my house." Of course what we mean is" if you are in the area CALL ME. And if I have time we will go out to eat or something." Well, in our experience here in North Africa, as well as with our Muslim friends in the States, they really mean it and if they live more than half hour from you don't be surprised if you are expected to spend the night!! Whatever time you go expect to stay a long time! You will most likely be shown every picture they have. And if they have a video of their wedding you will see that, too!

In our time here we have invited lots of our friends to our house. In this time I have learned a lot! How did I learn by inviting *our* friends to *our* house? Well, the first few times one of my friends was "invited" to our house she came in, went in the kitchen, and TOOK OVER! At first this got me a little upset. I was thinking, "Okay, this is my house, my kitchen, my food." Then I realized if I just accepted all the criticism I could really learn a lot. She means well when she tells me "You don't know how to do anything right!" I will admit they don't just pop anything into the oven directly from the freezer and eat it twenty minutes later, so I give them credit for that.

Every mother assumes the responsibility of teaching her daughters how to become good women. They are taught from the time they are little that is pleases God for them to be good housekeepers. The greatest compliment you can receive is, "You are a real woman." It is also an embarrassment to the woman of the family if her family eats out a lot. One embarrassing thing happened to me when we first got here. I was walking in the door to our apartment and my new friend (we had only been here a few weeks) stopped me and said, "Do you ever cook? I saw you just yesterday with a rotisserie chicken from the store. For us that is a Hashuma (a shameful thing.)"

Again this friend meant her comment for good. I explained to her that I really like to cook but we didn't have our kitchen set up yet. She nodded and later that day she rang our doorbell and handed us a huge plateful of food for our whole family! Later that week was when our daughter got sick. As soon as she knew we were at the hospital my friend walked in the rain to bring us food and see how we were doing. It is a real challenge for me to think of things I can do to repay my super hospitable friends and neighbors. Sadly, our hospitality is similar but our motives are completely different. While in my mind I do for others to show God's love for them, in their minds they do for others to gain God's love for themselves.

Healthy Version of Fish Tajine

Okay here is another recipe, only I modified it a little bit. A lot of oil is typically used in Tajines here, but since we eat them so often I try to adjust the recipe to make it a little better for us. If you want a more traditional tajine just add about a 1/4 cup more oil and spice mixture.

* A "Tajine" is a typical dish here. You can have tajine of chicken, fish, or meat. They are all prepared in a similar fashion.

INGREDIENTS:
(serves 4-5 people)

4 pieces of fish of your choice (frozen or fresh tilapia would be my choice if I lived in the USA)
2 potatoes
3 carrots
1 small onion (or less if you don't like onion very much)
2 medium sized tomatoes
1 handful of fresh chopped cilantro (or parsley)
1 tablespoon cumin
Salt to taste (a tablespoon maybe)
1 teaspoon black pepper
1/2 teaspoon ginger
1/2 teaspoon paprika
1/2 teaspoon saffron colorant
Chili pepper to taste
1/4 cup mixed veg. oil/ olive oil

Okay, it might seem a little intimidating with the spices but it isn't. And it is simple to make. Of course you don't have to eat it like the picture, you can serve it on individual plates!!!

1. Cut potatoes, onions, carrots, and tomatoes in 1/4 inch thick slices.
2. Layer all the above in a LARGE skillet or casserole dish if you would rather bake this dish. Potatoes first, ending with the tomato. Save a few slices of tomato.
3. Lay fish on top of veggies.
4. Mix together spices, 1/2 of the cilantro, oil and enough water so it pours easily over fish and lightly coats the top of the vegetables.
5. Place remaining tomatoes on top of the fish and sprinkle with remaining cilantro.
6. Add a light dusting of salt and cook until fish is fully cooked and potatoes and carrots are tender.

You may have to add more water, and change spices to your taste.

I hope you will try this recipe it is one of our favorites. I am jealous you guys won't have to be careful not to swallow any fish bones. It really is a pain to have a little tiny one stuck in your throat!

Feeling Alone

I just got off the phone with two of my good friends. I just got finished talking about all the hard things I feel I am facing right now. My husband just left for a trip for one week. So we are here alone for this short period of time during Ramadan. Ramadan is the time of the year when everyone suddenly becomes super spiritual. They all pray five times a day. They fast all day and then eat a ton at night. Of course that is loosely put.

I just complained and "vented" as we women like to say. Then I hung up the phone and God began to work in my heart. I know I am facing spiritual warfare right now. When I feel discontent I know it is because I am letting the devil win. I feel so convicted right now. Though I am facing challenges I have never faced before. Challenges I would not be facing if we did not live in a Muslim country. I am reminded that I **don't** understand. I don't have a clue what alone feels like. I just got off the phone with people telling me they were praying for me. I have many good friends who really do care about us who are praying for us. I am so thankful for them. I can't stop thinking about how it must be for the Christians here. Having to everyday be reminded that they don't fit in, even in the country where they were born. Let alone their families. The pressure they must feel. I am sure their families are asking them to pray and to go to the mosque. Some of them are completely alone. Like my friend Hayet who had no idea there were other Christians here for about eight years. That's "ALONE." But I don't feel sorry for them! Praise God, that is honestly the good kind of alone.

I am asking God to meet our needs and help us to be a blessing to those around us. Please pray for the Christians here. Pray for God to use them. Pray for God to strengthen and comfort them.

Respect is an Understatement.

I have been wanting to share this but I really haven't been able to think of the right words to say. Before we came over here, I will not try hiding the fact that I was scared. I was intimidated by what was in front of me. I felt so small and so helpless. I thought we would be hated and unwanted. I even let my mind entertain thought of all the horrible things that "could" happen to us. I made my self physically sick. Worry and fear- two things that don't have a place in the victorious Christian life were taking over.

After we got here and the Lord began a work in my heart everything was improving. I was learning to daily trust the Lord and not let myself think about anything "scary" or negative. Of course I had to learn to not watch Aljezeira News Station, and we quickly deleted all the propaganda channels. There is one channel that shows nothing but insurgents in Iraq killing American Soldiers and laughing about it. They just show it over and over again all day. Yea, sick to your stomach doesn't explain what I felt when I saw that. We erased that one as quickly as possible. I had to eliminate as much negative as I could. But everyday I was growing daily more comfortable here.

Then we heard news from Turkey. A Bible publishing warehouse had basically been attacked. There had been five young Turkish guys who claimed they wanted to learn more about Jesus and His message. They arranged a meeting with two young Turkish Christians and a German man serving in Turkey. They used the publishing place as a meeting center as well. Well, to make the story short and less graphic, the five "seekers" brutally killed the two young Christians and their German mentor. The German man had a wife and three beautiful children. He was in his 30's I think. They had a huge funeral for the men. Thousands of Turkish believers attended. The fiancé of one of the young Turks had to watch the funeral from far away because, though she is a Christian, her parents are not and would not let her attend.

The thing that impacted me the most about all of this and the thing that really helped change me, was that at this funeral the wife of the German was interviewed. She was asked if she had anything to say to the men who did this to her husband. She replied to the question with a very short but familiar statement: "Father, forgive them for they know not what they have done." She responded in Turkish. I am sure when the people heard her answer they were amazed and confused. This response can only be given and understood by those who know the love and forgiveness of Jesus Christ.

When I heard about this I began to cry, I asked God to make me as strong as she is. She stayed in Turkey with her family. This kind of example I have never seen before. I praised God that his grace is sufficient. I learned how petty the little things I get upset about are. I learned honestly how to appreciate my husband more. I learned that if this lady could trust God and have faith even enough to stay there, that God would meet all my needs and calm all my fears.

I am not saying since then that I do not struggle or worry. It would be a lie to say that. Since then I realized that my life is about God. He is great and He will always be all I need! I can honestly say that living here has changed me in ways I never thought possible. I know God is working in my heart and life. It is amazing to me that if you are scared and alone and if you search for Him, He not only lets you find Him but He lets you know Him better. Never more than a few days go by without me thinking about this lady. I don't even know her name I just know that I respect her and that God has greatly used her in my life. I just wanted to share this with whoever is reading.

So, what's for dinner tonight?
Well, if you are from here chances are you had **Harira.** This is a famous soup that the people here eat every night to break the Ramadan fast. I thought it would be appropriate to share the recipe. If you make it then you will know exactly what this whole country smells like from about 4:00pm until 7:30pm. I open the door to our apartment and I feel like I just took a bite. Every family eats it

everyday. I am not exaggerating. If they don't eat it everyday they are really in the minority. So here you go, you can fit right in.

Ingredients:
1/2 cup Chickpeas (garbanzo beans)
1/4 cup lentils
2Tbsp chopped parsley
2Tbsp chopped cilantro
1 small chopped onion
1/2 tsp black pepper
1/2 tsp saffron colorant
Three sticks of celery chopped very fine
(It would be great if you could use the leafy part too)
1/2 tsp turmeric
1lb lamb or beef chopped small
2 cubes beef bullion
3 Tbsp olive oil
1/4 cup rice
8 grated tomatoes
Salt to taste
1/4 cup flour mixed with 1/2 cup water
Place all the first section of ingredients in a large pot, sauté on medium heat for a few minutes. Fill your pot 2/3 of the way full with water. Cook until all ingredients are tender.
Add in rice, tomatoes, and salt*. Cook on low until rice is tender. (You can also add 1/4 cup vermicelli pasta for a fuller soup.)
Finally add flour and water mixture. Simmer for a while longer until all is well blended.
*Add lemon juice to taste for a real authentic taste.
This recipe serves about 6 people.
* salt and lemon are always placed on the table for everyone to add to their personal taste. Harira is usually served needing salt. So don't over do it with the salt in the pot.
Let me be honest.... it is good...but to eat it everyday for a month.... well....

I mean it is not Papa John's, or El Rancho Grande, or even Taco Bell, or The Cheesecake Factory, or Starbucks, or Applebee's, or Cinnabon, or Cracker Barrel, or even Subway...Okay, sorry...it has been a while

Can't we all just get along?

I had heard before I came that during Ramadan sometimes there are more fights than usual. Let me say TRUE, TRUE, TRUE. Fighting is kind of a common thing to see on the streets from time to time here. But in the past few days I have seen two pretty major ones. The other day my husband and I were shopping in a busy area of town and we saw a huge swarm of people gathering around a group of men fighting. Now swarms are super common. Crowds are everywhere here. But when there is a fight **everyone** goes to see what is happening.

So we were in the busy area of town shopping, we got in our car and we were trying to drive away. The mass of people was screaming, women were grabbing their children and running. I looked over and to my surprise the men were throwing huge rocks at each other. I mean softball size. They were throwing them at a man on the ground too. All the cars were honking like crazy, more crazy than normal, trying to get away from the rocks and the fight. I know that is not normal for here, I was just amazed it could go on for so long. We were stuck in traffic at the intersection for at least 10 minutes, and the fighting was not letting up.

Just last night I heard yelling outside our apartment. I mean hateful yelling. I looked down to see what was going on. It was almost 1 am. All the men that worked at the barbershop on the first floor of our apartment were in a fight with some men dressed in djellabas and long beards. I looked around and noticed almost every balcony had someone leaning over watching the fight. Live entertainment! Honestly all this anger scares me. I have seen several other small fights this month as well. You know they will blame it on the lack of food all day or whatever, but it is the lack of Jesus Christ in their hearts. I guess I would be mad and frustrated all the time if I was living only for myself and trying to work my way into Heaven. They say Islam is the true religion of peace. Hmmmm.

Thank You!

Hey, I just wanted to write a quick post to say thank you to all my friends who called and e-mailed or posted comments in this time while my husband was away. I feel very blessed to have so many true friends. Thank you for your prayers and concern for me. I know people are honestly praying for us and that is such an awesome thing! Thank you very much!!

October

Spices and Things

I was just thinking you women might want to know where we do our grocery shopping. I remember when my husband came here to visit before we came, one of my first questions was, "So how's the shopping?" I wanted to know how modern the markets were.

Well, it turns out here we have one extreme to the other. Below our apartment on the first floor of the apartment building across form ours is a supermarket much like an American grocery store. Our other option (the more exciting and interesting option) is to walk a few blocks to the suq. A "suq" is an open-air market. Or to be more exact is a very crowded street that transforms into a market. It is packed with carts with fresh vegetables and fruits. Then little stores line the street selling live chickens, spices, beans, toiletry items, and really just about anything you can think of. There are little "hole in the wall" stores packed with imported stuff from Europe. Things are only sometimes cheaper in the "suq". Still the majority of the people do there shopping there. I guess out of tradition. I do about half and half.

When it rains the suq becomes one nasty place. The particular suq we go to is on a hill. The area where they sell the fish is near the top of the hill. When you buy fish they gut it for you, throwing the guts on the ground. When it rains everything washes down stream! So you can smell and see fish guts all threw the fruit and vegetable section! Obviously here there are no clean ups on isle 5! Pretty gross! On a good day however, the smells and colors are beautiful. This is a picture of a little spice stand. Everything is always fresh. These spices make our little glass bottled ones taste so dull and stale.

Bad Timing

Last night we had a few people over for dinner. So we were finishing up and I noticed that we had a lot of chocolate cake left over. I put it on a plate and thought it would be really nice to share it with my friends who live down stairs. They love our American desserts because they are sweeter than their traditional ones. So I grabbed the plate and headed down the elevator. I left my husband and everyone else talking at the table knowing I would only be a few minutes. My friends knew we had guests.

I rang the doorbell and our friend's maid answered the door. Their house was very dark and quiet in a strange kind of way. She invited me in. She looked very hesitant, like she didn't know what to do or where to take me. Normally I would have been warmly greeted a few moments after entering by a few members of the family. I looked around and quickly saw everyone. There they were, all of them, all the women of the family completely covered being lead in prayer by their father. To make it a little stranger for me, when Muslims pray they must pray in the direction of Mecca, so they were all facing the doorway I was standing in. I am sure they saw me, but they didn't even lift one eye in my direction. I stood still for a few awkward minutes and then I turned to the maid. I am not sure if I forced her to interrupt her prayers or not. I told her I needed to go. I was really wishing she had never opened the door. This morning my friend called me and thanked me for the cake. She didn't mention my untimely visit. Before Ramadan this particular friend almost never spoke about Islam. I am not even sure if she prayed, but during Ramadan their prayers "count" for more points.

Now all the stores are starting advertise all the traditional clothing and party type foods, because Ramadan will be over in a little more than a week and everyone is getting ready for the big bash they have to celebrate the end of fasting. Believe me I will be celebrating too, because I will be so glad when Ramadan is OVER!!

Playing Mosque

Or should I say "playing Imam." Tonight right before the call to pray at sunset, I heard two of our young neighbors who are maybe ten years old or so, out on their balcony screaming the call to prayer. "Allah hu Akbar" They where screaming it, and then cracking up. Their screaming was quickly followed by their mother screaming at them to stop. I heard her saying, "You boys have to stop now. Now!! Stop it now!!" I couldn't help but laugh. I quickly ducked behind the clothes I was hanging so no one could see the foreign lady laughing

140

at this little innocent mocking of their precious call to one of their mandatory duties! I found the whole situation quite funny!

You mean you can't stay for dinner?
On Saturday one of my closest friends here invited me to her house to eat the meal at sunset. I agreed to go and I was excited to be invited to eat with her and some of her cousins who are also friends of mine. We were out shopping half the day on Saturday to prepare for the meal. We also stopped by the tailors to pick up our new djellabas we had made. I always have a great time with her.

Last night after we got home form our church, which is an hour and a half away, I went to her house. It was very close to the time to eat and everyone was already sitting in around the table with Harira in their bowls. I think it is hilarious, as soon as they her hear the first part of the word "Allah..." they already have their food in their mouths. I hid my smile and reached for my spoon. So we ate, and we ate, and we ate some more. The word you say when you are telling someone to eat is "kul" like "cool". So, I think I heard them telling me to "kul" about 100 times. I think I said "Safee" which means "enough" about 200 times. One way or another I was still left with that never-ending bowl of soup!!!

After we were all stuffed they all got up to go pray. One at a time they went into the dark living room and wrapped blankets around themselves and read the Koran and prayed. They had to do it that way so I wasn't left alone. I could tell my friend was a little nervous about leaving me but her Mom told her she would sit with me. After about 20 minutes of this everyone had finished and they were lying all over the couches. I tucked my feet up under me and watched a ridiculous TV program in Arabic. I was glad it was in this dialect of Arabic. I understood enough to know it was a really cheesy comedy.

After what I thought was long enough I stood up and stretched my arms up over my head, and stating how tired I was. I told my friends I had to go. It was after 9:00 pm. Then the protests began. "You mean you are not staying for dinner? My mom is about to begin preparing it." I didn't know what to do. Quickly remembering the honor/shame culture here, I told them "You must understand, my children are with my husband and it is a shame to me to have him caring for them for such a long time!" They began to nod reluctantly.

I apologized for having to leave the extremely exciting naptime and then I left. As you can see I am applying what I am learning about the culture here. :)

GREAT TIME

My friends here are all very different. I always have a wonderful time hanging out with each one of them. I practice my Arabic with them, go shopping with them, learn about the culture from them, and learn about their religion from them. That last point is where the problem begins. I learn by asking questions. I listen to their answers and then I always try to share things about what I believe with them. I share with them about the freedoms I have in Christ. They have a very hard time listening to this. I was questioning one of my friends about why she changed only during Ramadan. Why the head covering and long sleeves during the day and then hair down with a sleeveless dress at night? Why only pray faithfully one month out of the year?

I have shared with many of my friends that true believers and followers of Jesus Christ are always the same. If I think it is right to do I need to do it everyday all day long. They see the obvious contradiction and just shrug their shoulders. They feel obligated to do everything they do. They all say the love Ramadan. Sometimes I find that really hard to believe.

I would like to ask you pray that the Lord would open up more doors for me to talk to them about Him. I always have fun with them. They are great people. I just hate thinking about their eternity. It would be easy for me to just hang out with them, but I know hanging out will leave blood on my hands. It can be intimidating, to say the least, to bring up conversations that single me out and that magnify our differences. But it is true: our differences go far beyond my blue eyes.

"I JUST SAID THAT! Didn't I?"

Okay, so I would not be covering all the bases if I did not write about torture...I mean LANGUAGE SCHOOL! I am in language school here learning dialectal Arabic. Arabic as you may know is not written using "our" letters so this really complicates things! So in other words, it is not like how it was when I was in Spanish language school. There I would just write down the new word in a small notebook. In Arabic there are sounds we don't have letters for!

For example the H in English, "H-h-h-Hat" right? Well, here we need to learn three ways to pronounce what to me always sounds like "H". There is a sound that is kind of like a "KH".... but honestly it sounds like somebody clearing his or her throat. Then I was taught another "H" sound. It has to come from deep in you lungs. When our teachers teach us they always put their hands on their upper chests and ask us to do the same. They say we should be feeling vibration. Hmm.

Today, I probably repeated a word 25 times after my teacher because I just could not hear the difference in what he was saying as opposed to what I was saying! AHH! Talk about frustrating, I kept telling everybody, "I just said that!" It was pretty funny. Our two other friends in class with me were agreeing with me. Nice to have the support. Our teacher was cracking up shaking his head, "no".

It is NOT easy learning a new language ever. If you have children I think things can even get a little trickier. Not to mention annoying when your three year old can pronounce Arabic letters better than you and all your friends LOVE to point that out. God is giving me the patience and the desire to learn. Little by little everyday that is my goal. When I was ending Spanish language school I realized how much I did not know when I was suppose to be "finished" learning. The truth is I am still learning English. I like to look at learning new languages as a journey. It seems to be easier to grasp that way. Really, though it is not easy and sometimes I have to make myself leave my children and go to school. I know it is an awesome opportunity from God to be able to learn how to communicate His word with people who otherwise might not hear. But please pray for me!

"You are the KING!"

We all know that God loves it when we sing to Him and Praise Him. I just can't help but think He must enjoy it even more to hear those praises in Arabic. Sometimes when the Christians here are singing at church I feel tears coming to my eyes. There is one song they sing that I can understand almost completely. I love it. It is the song they sing to Jesus and say, "You are our King." It is beautiful. They sing it with joy and thankfulness.

I have written several posts in a negative tone about Ramadan. Today I was thinking of something that has really blessed me this month. That being, while most people here are following strict Muslim practices and talking about all the things they are obligated to do, the Christians are learning about and experiencing even more the freedom they have in Christ. For example, yesterday, it was awesome when our friend who was visiting us understood that he didn't have to fast during Ramadan. A little funny too! Tomorrow Ramadan is over and everyone will be stuffing their faces all day. I am pretty excited myself. It will be nice to get things back to normal. Normal? I guess that wasn't the right word, back to the way things were before Ramadan.

Babies and HOT Peppers

One thing I noticed after a little while of being here is that they don't sell too many high chairs. For the reason that if they did their baby would be sitting up way higher than everyone else. People here eat sitting on the couches they have lining their living rooms. They usually hold the small children on their laps or they just let the kids run around like crazy. Whenever we eat with other people, someone always insists on holding our daughter while we eat. I am never comfortable with that situation. You know being the typical mother, I worry she is going to spill something or break something. I also worry about what they might feed her. Well, the other night I had a reason to fear! Our friend wanted to hold our daughter at the table. She seemed to like him so we started eating with her eating sitting with him. There was a small bowl of extremely HOT sauce on the table. If you have ever been in South America, it was similar to Peruvian Aji. We are talking about super HOT. This stuff makes the hot sauce at Mexican restaurants seem like ketchup.

So, you probably know where I am going with this, our friend had no idea how HOT it was. He took a small piece of bread and scooped up the HOT sauce and popped it right in our daughter's little mouth. I didn't know how to say anything in Arabic at that moment. I screamed "NO!" Everyone at the table was running around trying to get something to wipe it out of her mouth and soothe the burning. She was shocked at the new, horrible taste in her mouth. I think it was the worst ten minutes of her little life. Our friend felt awful. We assured him she was okay. He learned that night that babies aren't too fond of hot sauce. As for me, I have learned in my short time being a mom in living in three different countries and traveling to many more that I can't shelter my kids. I can't keep them from being right in there with everything the country and the culture have to offer.

Obviously it is not always easy for me or for them but I really believe if you want to build relationships with people you have to share your life. Later that night our daughter was sitting with our friend playing on the floor, forgetting all about her experience at the dinner table.

So...uh...where's the bathroom?

We just got back from a trip around the country. We traveled to meet new believers and others who are searching for the truth. We drove all day on Tuesday and made a stop to give some materials to a young guy who wants to study more of God's Word. We were with him for a few hours and then it was back in the car again. We had a good friend of ours Ahmed with us who is a new believer himself. He was such an encouragement to us. He and my husband talked nearly the entire trip about Jesus and The Bible. He is excited to know that he now has the truth. It seems like all this guy does is read the Bible!!! Even in the car. When there was a break in the conversation he was reading his New Testament. I felt sick at even the thought of reading in the car on those winding roads.

As we continued driving, it was getting late. Ahmed mentioned that we were relatively close to the "city" where his family lives. Or to explain it better, the tiny little village very far away from everything where he grew up. Let's just say I can see why he lives in the city now! We were so close he suggested that we stay in the village with his family. So we continued on. First we came to the turn off of the main road. There was a sign there for the next city so I thought we didn't have much farther to go. Wrong! After passing through a very small city the road got extremely narrow and dark. We went further on the loosely paved road. After maybe 1/2 hour I saw faint lights in the distance. Honestly, at that point I was relieved to know that they at lest had electricity! We soon parked our car and grabbed all our belongings and began the walk to his house.

145

It was incredibly dark. Finally we arrived at his home made of mud and brick walls. His super nice family welcomed us in. We sat on blankets spread out on the ground and ate in their home. Their house is made up of two rooms that are connected by a metal awning. You have to go outside to get from one room to the other. They have a dirt floor, two light bulbs hanging down, and NO bathroom. Not even an outhouse! So it was a different experience for us to say the least. Honestly, I had a great time. I am thankful the Lord is allowing me these opportunities. The time at their house was awesome for language practice and learning about a culture very different from the culture of the "city people" here in this country.

We all wore the same clothes the entire time we were there, partly for lack of place to change and also because they would find it strange if we changed our clothes everyday. I have to be honest, when I asked to go to the bathroom and was lead down a dark path... I started to get frustrated. I thought about how I didn't want to be there. I stopped and asked God to help me, to help me appreciate these people, their way of life, the hard work they do everyday, and their hospitality to us. God answered my prayer. We had a wonderful time. I can say it was truly by God's grace!

Frustration

When I mention frustration I am sure everyone thinks I am referring to my own frustration. Not the case this time! I am referring to the frustration of my three year old. Yesterday I was busy putting up the summer clothes and taking out the fall and winter clothes. My son came in the room and asked for some juice. I told him to go ask Fatima. She is the girl who watches the kids while we go to language school. I heard him searching all around the apartment for her.

After a few minutes he returned. He told me she wasn't here any more. I laughed and again instructed him to go find her and ask her, because I was up to my ears in little kids clothes! Again I heard him screaming, "Fatima, Fatima, FA-TI-MA." A few seconds later I heard the door to his room open and I heard him talking. He ran into my room and very upset told me that Fatima was on the ground. He proceeded to get down and demonstrate exactly how she was positioned on the ground. He had been in there with her for a few minutes, right in front of her. He could not understand why she would not respond to him. He was very upset. I quietly explained to him that she was praying. Well, not really praying...more like reciting. Try explaining how some praying is good and some bad to a three year old!

I was a little surprised she wouldn't even acknowledge his presence in the room. He has so many questions. It is a little difficult to teach our kids that Islam is wrong without teaching them to be intolerant. For example the Mosques here are such beautiful buildings and they have tall minarets, some with crescent moon shapes on top. My son thinks they are fascinating. Once when he asked to go there, I tried to simplify the reason why we would not be going by simply stating that Mosques are "BAD." Well, it's true they are, but does that make the people who go there bad? You can imagine the questions that came from my simple answer. I know this is just the beginning of the challenges we will face with our children living here. I would appreciate your prayers for wisdom in this area! I have a very curious little boy!

November

Such a spiritual thing to do

Today I had a really disturbing experience! I went to practice Arabic with my friend at her store. I usually go and just sit and talk with her for an hour or so. She is rather forceful with correcting me so really she is just what I need! Anyway, first I should in saying I went to her "store" I am being really generous with that word. Her "store" is the size of a small bathroom. So, we were just sitting there talking, as women do best, when these SUPER MUSLIMS came in. You know, the fully-covered, can't-see-their-face, all-black type. I always feel like they think I am dressed awful or that my hair is just creating such a problem here. So I am always uncomfortable around them.

Well, they were especially strange because they came in asking to see the clothes that were hung up directly over our heads. They were hovering. I hate when people hover. They were almost leaning on me. (People here have no concept of the whole personal space idea.) As my friend and I were helping get down the clothes that they supposedly wanted to see, evidently in that moment the lady was not focused on the clothes as we were, because they STOLE MY PURSE! They were gone about two minutes when I noticed my bag was not were I had left it, which was about an arms reach from me. I was shocked! I am not going to lie. I was super MAD! So many thoughts were racing through my mind. I felt so taken advantage of.

It is hard sometimes to think good of people especially when you get burned like that. The crazy thing was that it was head covered women, not "worldly" women. I was robbed by supposed the example of spirituality. I asked my friend this question," So I am a foreigner and follower of Jesus. NOT a Muslim. You want to me to like and respect your religion when my things just got stolen from the most spiritual among you?" She was quiet, her usually holier-than-thou answers didn't seem to flow in this situation. I explained that though I was upset it was only things that I lost and things are not what bring happiness.

To be honest when things like this happen, I get mad. I really lose compassion for the people here. It is easy to do. They are so aggressive and critical. I always have to keep reminding myself that they really don't know any better. They have NO hope and nothing to live for. My husband reminded me as we were walking down the street with me crying after the whole ordeal that God has given us so much and I have to be an example of His Grace. It is humbling. I just wanted to be mad at that lady. I wanted to take out all my feelings of frustration with this culture on her. I wanted to go off about hypocrisy and about how everything they do is for show.

My flesh is so weak. Praise God, He helped me overcome all my anger towards them. (For today, I have to seek continually to know the mind of Christ.) I know that lady, as well as all the other Muslims, just needs Jesus. Only by His blood can they have a new life. Only by the Word can they really learn how to fear God and live Holy lives. I can't expect honesty and peace.

My House, My Rules

Two days ago I had a conversation. It was around 7:30 at night and one of my "friends" came to visit me. We made the first required half hour of small talk and then she started in on me. She has always tries to convince me to convert to Islam. She always begins the same way...."we are the same, we both love God", etc. I always struggle to get a word in. She is in her 40's and twice my size with a very forceful type personality. She has a very argumentative way about her in her conversation style. This is always very frustrating for me.

So, this time I with the courage that only God can give I let her have it, so to speak. I was speaking in a tone I rarely use. I told her, "Excuse me, this is MY house and you are NOT going to come here and talk at me. If you are going to continue to sit here I get to talk and you get to LISTEN." I went on to question her about the "peace" and "liberty" she talks about in her religion? "So what I am seeing in Iran is liberty???"(In Iran, it has been reported that women are being arrested for exposing an inch of their hair or wearing too bright of colors.) And what about Jihad? "Is that the peace you are talking about?" Or course she was trying desperately to stop me so she could speak but I just continued while my heart pounded and the feeling of anxiety probably very obvious in my voice. I could feel my face and neck were red hot.

I continued by addressing her favorite topic: Our Bible has been corrupted. She is always saying this. I told her to show me when and how it has been corrupted, I told her I needed an answer outside of the Koran. Then from there we began to talk about a how I have read the Koran and how she doesn't have a clue about the true Words of Jesus. I asked her why she is afraid to read the New Testament? Why is the Arabic Bible illegal here? I explained that in my country we have the freedom to search out the truth and that I did just that. I became a Christian when I was 17 so it is easy for me to explain how we are not born followers of Jesus. I explained that every person who is a true follower of Jesus Christ makes that choice for himself. I again let her know that I have read a good portion of the Koran and I STILL believe the Words of Jesus. I challenged her to read the New Testament and to compare the lives and teachings of Jesus to that of Mohammed.

I paused to let her speak. I had to take a break. She honestly didn't have much to say. I had gone to the bedroom to get her a New Testament. . I laid it on the table and explained it was a gift from me to her. She picked it up and looked at it. She was quiet. I saw her struggle for what to say next. After a few minutes I guess she realized she had to change the subject, so what does she start in on? President Bush and how all the problems in entire world are caused by AMERICA. After much reasoning she agreed with me that there is absolutely nothing she or I could do about the problems in Iraq, Afghanistan, or Palestine. WOW. I was shocked that we agreed on something. We talked peacefully for a while longer and when she was leaving she thanked me over and over again for the New Testament. She kissed it and touched it to her heart. She left with the Word of God in her purse and questions in her mind.

"So THAT'S why you guys have so many Bibles!"

I am so excited as I write this! Yesterday God gave me an awesome opportunity to share the Gospel from start to finish with Fatima. She works in our house watching our children when we go to language school. She is usually a very hard case to crack. She rarely smiles and anytime I say anything about Jesus she is super fast with something about Mohammad. She fasted extra days after Ramadan to earn more points with God. When I have talked with her in the past she has always had a little smirk on her face and pitiful-type little look every time I mess up my Arabic.

150

But PRAISE GOD, not yesterday! It began while she was helping me go through a lesson in my language schoolbook. While we read many names we have in both Arabic and English (OT names), she asked me if we name our boys Issa (the Muslim name for Jesus which is not the same as Yesua El Mesih -Jesus the Messiah. A little confusing I know.) Anyway, I told her we don't name our boys His name because there is no one like Him. And no man deserves His honorable name. She shook her head in agreement. She then said, "I will not name my son Mohammad because you are right." And so our conversation went out of our language schoolbook to the names of God, to rights of citizenship. Why you ask? Because if she has a baby in the USA her baby is a citizen of both America and this country. If I have a baby here my baby is American only. This is a Muslim country and they want to keep it that way. I am always talking about how in the USA we have Christians, Muslims, Hindus, etc.

I explained all this obvious oppression in her country while saying "I'm sorry." over and over. You can say anything as long as you apologize here! She was extremely interested. So, I took it a step farther. "In my country and in South America were I lived we have the freedom to study and learn about other religions, to go to any Mosque or Church or Temple we choose." I explained how I am not allowed into the Mosque here. She was shocked. I told her about how in America you can buy huge beautiful Korans and tons of books about Islam. Or course she thought that was great. Then I told her that the thing that hurts my heart is that if I were to lose my Bible I could not even buy a new one. She reasoned," Oh, because you want it in English or Spanish." I stopped her, "No, because you can't buy a Bible of any kind here." (I didn't want to go into the fact they are illegal.) She then started smiling...."Oh, now I understand why you all have so many Bibles, because your husband has the tendency to lose things."

From there I got to share with her how we both believe that Jesus is coming back. I explained that Jesus DID die (Muslims don't believe Jesus died. They believe He was called up to Heaven.) She surprised me by asking "WHY?" I explained everything to her. Near the end of our conversation I asked her if she had ever eaten food from Turkey. She told me "No." I then asked her if it was good or not? She laughed and told me she didn't know. She knew exactly what I was getting at. She told me food is like religion. You can't know the truth until you "try" it. She left promising to read the NT I had given her awhile back. I told her to begin with John and Romans. Please pray that she does. Tomorrow or the next day I am planning to show her The Jesus Film in this dialect of Arabic. PLEASE PRAY! When she left yesterday she thanked me for our conversation and told me she knew it was very important. She told me she loved me as a sister. I was shocked; all this from the girl who prays in my son's room and always has a stone cold face.

Cesar

From Cesar's Blog in Spanish
www.luzamusulmanes.blogspot.com

Ahmed

Yesterday I went to visit a friend of mine, named Ahmed, and we talked a good while about Islam and Christianity. It was Friday, and like every Friday it was a special day for the Muslims – the day of prayer – so Ahmed only opened his business for a few hours. While we talked he told me that all Muslims say that the Qur'an contains everything in it; it has the Law of Moses in it, the Psalms, the gospel, and the revelations of Muhammad.

They are extremely proud about what their book has in it, even though the Qur'an doesn't really contain the gospel or any of the others in it. That's just what they have been made to believe themselves. It is sad to see how the enemy has done such an efficient job in deceiving these people with such a strong spiritual blindness.
We will continue to talk about the Savior with the world. We only ask that you continue praying for the Muslim world.

'Lailat Al Qadr'

Of the 355 days in the Islamic lunar calendar, 'Lailat Al Qadr' (The Night of Design or Destiny) is the most important for Muslims. According to the religion, it is better than a thousand months or more than 30 thousand regular nights. This same night over 1300 years ago, Muhammad received his first revelation. Almost all of the Muslim scholars agree that it was between the 26th and 27th of Ramadan, which ends up being October 8th and 9th of this year.

While talking to my teacher, I found out that for the Muslims today is the day when:
-Muhammad first received the Qur'an.
-The heavens are opened for the prayers of the Muslim people.
-One prayer today is equal to the accumulative prayers of 1,000 months.

-If you have a problem with another person you need to go to him and try to make things right.
-The entire family goes to the mosque and prays – women upstairs, men downstairs.
-People will be praying in their local mosque all day and night.
-Those that don't normally pray throughout the year will make it a priority on this day.

Looking at this it is easy to see that the people here are looking for a way to get to heaven. Unfortunately, they are going down the wrong path. Many pray on this day and will continue to pray because they may not really have a desire to pray throughout the rest of the year. This is the day when you can really rack up points on your prayer account if you have been slacking before and if you haven't been living a good life, it's a good time to start.

My Religion is the Best in the World

Last night around 9:45 P.M. my wife and I were out looking for a house, and as we were going through downtown a few men began to talk to us, eventually asking if we were fasting like the rest of them for Ramadan. I told him that we were Christians and explained how we also fast.

Toward the end of the conversation one of the men told me that Muslims have the best religion in the world. He was really excited to talk to me and told me that I needed to become a Muslim. I only asked him, "Why do you say that Islam is the best religion in the world?" He didn't say a word – the silence was almost deafening. He couldn't give me a single reason why he made such a claim.

Many Muslims have the same reaction as he did. They are left without a concrete answer to such a question. A lot of the people are only followers of the religion because of their family and their reputation publicly and privately has to be guarded. As absurd as it may sound, most are wrapped up in this religion because they want to maintain honor.

Pray for these needy people. Many go through the actions of a Muslim like a robot, obeying and doing exactly as they have been told. It's almost as if they don't have the right to think for themselves. Islam has blinded them.

Don't Say That God Wants to Speak with You

These were the exact words that a friend of mine told me after I read a short message to him that I had prepared. I prayed over the message and worked on it for a while so I could share it with my wife and co-workers here in North Africa. Before preaching it, I went out into the street where my friend was to share it with him and hopefully get his help with my pronunciation. I really wanted him to be honest with me as he corrected my Arabic. I began with reading the first line, which said, "I received Christ as my Savior when I was ten years old." He just stared at me and said nothing. I asked him if what I said made sense, and he told me, "yeah," so I continued. I was pretty excited about actually making it that far without a mistake.

I asked him later on in the message, "Do you understand what I'm saying?" he said, "Yeah, keep going." Eventually, I came to a part that said, "We are already God's. We should understand that God wants to speak with us and in return we should speak with Him."

Immediately, his face changed. I looked at him, and I said, "Okay, I guess I've made a mistake here. I either wrote something incorrectly or my pronunciation was off." He snapped back, "Don't say that God wants to speak with you. Cesar, you need to understand that God is the creator of everything, and the truth is, we are nothing. Why would God want to speak with you? How could you say something like that?"

When I heard that, I realized right away what the god of Islam is like a separated God. One that always carries a rod of chastisement, who has no desire to speak with his people. A god that spoke through a false prophet, Muhammad, and won't speak to anyone else until we arrive at the judgment.

What a misconception of the true God! This is what they believe their god is like. They have no idea that they can have a personal relationship with the God of heaven. No conversation with Him is even remotely possible in their minds. The sad truth is, that they will continue believing this if we do not rise up quickly and take the gospel to them.

The Welcome
(From Mariet, Cesar's wife)

155

I had only been living in North Africa for a few weeks when at the store I ran into a woman who lived two doors down from me at the time. I had seen her before, but not in the same place. In public, she wore her djellaba, fully clothed from head to toe, with a veil that allowed me to only see her eyes. She was a true Muslim in every sense of the word.

She greeted me in Arabic, and I responded. I had only been studying the language for about a week and a half at the time, but she just kept on talking to me in Arabic. Finally, I told her that I had just recently started learning Arabic. When she heard this, she told me to repeat the phrase she was saying. I began to repeat what she was saying and didn't understand a word of what I was saying until I heard her say the name "Muhammad." Then it hit me! She was trying to get me to repeat the "Shahada," which states, "There is no god but Allah, and Muhammad is his prophet." Evidently, if a person repeats this three times that individual is publicly recognized as a Muslim and one who has rejected Jesus Christ, the Son of God.

As soon as I realized what was going on, I told her that I was sorry, but I just couldn't repeat that. I said goodbye, and it was then that she spoke to me in Spanish. She knew Spanish! She could have spoken with me in my own language from the beginning of our conversation if she wanted, but nevertheless, she chose to speak with me in Arabic just to get me to repeat after her without me knowing what I was saying.

Well, I didn't repeat the "Shahada" three times, but the whole ordeal scared me a little. I left the store as quickly as I could and met up with my husband to tell him everything that had just happened.

Index

First Adam, Second Adam
Sharing Christ with a Muslim in two simple lessons

Often we dive in and learn a boatload about the Koran and the beliefs of the Muslims around the world but when it comes to sitting down and sharing the message of hope with an honest, seeking Muslim we are not sure where to start. After all, it is a big book! Here is one idea. I am writing this as if I am talking to a Muslim. The parenthesis is to you. There are only two lessons here for a number of reasons. First, to cover the whole Bible from Adam to Jesus will be too much to take in at one time. Attention will be lost and the Spirit won't have a chance to convict the hearer of the important foundational truths of the Word. Second, it will give you an excuse to test their sincerity by meeting a second time. Third, the gospel is arrived at fairly quickly, two meetings, in order to begin answering their subsequent questions. Forth, two lessons are easy for any Christian to memorize and teach. Some series go for 10 lessons or more. Most can't remember or concentrate for that long.

Lesson 1

To understand Christ and the reason he had to come to earth to die for our sins, you will have to first get an understanding of God from the very beginning (Muslims believe in all the prophets but have all their stories wrong. To start at the beginning is to begin to correct all the wrong perversions of the stories from the first). In Genesis 1 the Bible says that God created the heavens and the earth. On the sixth day he created man and saw that everything was good. The Bible says that God created man in his image. He created man with a spirit (Muslims believe that man has an eternal spirit. They don't have the concept of a living or dead spirit. Here you can establish the existence of a living spirit with in them personally). To make that spirit live within man, God breathed his own breathe in Adam. God created Adam and Eve to have a personal relationship with them (Islam has no idea of a personal relationship with God. Since God created us to need a relationship with him, this will begin to meet that need.) There was no sin in the garden. Everything was perfect.

God only made one rule: don't eat of the tree of the knowledge of good and evil. God only made one punishment: In the day that you eat of that tree you will die. (You must lay the groundwork well, that one sin brings death. Not the common Muslim idea that the books kept in heaven must tilt in your favor.)

In Chapter 3 Satan enters the picture. He takes his first steps to trick man with this lie: in the day that you eat, you will not die! After Adam and Eve had both sinned against God by eating of the tree, God came looking for them as he always did in the garden. But they had hid themselves in shame. The judgment for their sin was death. Their relationship with God was broken. (Your Muslim friend needs to understand that he has a personal spirit that has been separated from God. The Muslims think in groups. However, the spirit is in an individual and he must make an individual decision to accept or reject God's Word.) Their spirit that had been made to live by the breath of God was dead on the moment of sin. Their bodies would soon follow in death.

God, however, loved the man and woman so much that from the very beginning God provided a way to take away their sin (Islam does not teach that God loves man). God killed a sheep, his own creation. (The major reason that Muslims cannot understand that Christ would have died is because Christ was God's prophet in their book. Christ to us is God's Son. "How could God let his Son die?" This can be understood by seeing how God killed his own creation first because of his love for man.) He took the skin of that sheep and covered the shame of sin of the man: his nakedness. He even made a promise to Satan. Though Satan had conquered the spirit of man with Sin, God would send the seed of the woman to bruise the head of Satan.

From Adam, the first man and prophet, the command was given to yearly sacrifice the blood of a sheep. The Muslims have a yearly festival called the "Aid el-kabir". They kill a lamb per family just like the Jews did. Another thing that Mohammed borrowed from the Jews. Some North African Berber tribes even take the blood and put it on their door just like the Jewish Passover Feast. They don't believe that this lamb is a sacrifice for sin. They can see however in

158

the OT how every sacrifice of a lamb was for the covering of sin. The death of that sacrifice would cover the sin of the man as they waited for the promise that God had told them would come: the seed of man who would bruise Satan's head.

In Isaiah 53 the prophet gives us further details about who this seed of the woman would be. He would be bruised for our iniquities. He would be taken to his death silently as a sheep goes to the sheerer. He would forever take our sin from us. (A crucial truth that will lead to the conversion of a Muslim is when they realize all the prophesize that Christ fulfilled. The more the better.)

It only takes one sin to deserve death. God cannot forgive that sin in your life because that sin caused the death of your spirit. The only thing that can make your spirit live again is to transfer your sin onto someone else.

Lesson 2

John chapter 3 brings all of this foundational teaching about God, the judgment of sin, the death of the spirit, etc into the life of Christ. The major points to hit in this session are:

1. Every man must be born again in the spirit.
2. The new birth creates a new man with a new family: the family of God.
3. Jesus, the Word of God, came as God's final sacrificial lamb.

This should give you an idea of how you can approach a Muslim when God gives you the opportunity. Many have tested this with Muslims in the Muslim world.

Personal Involvement

Interested in becoming a missionary to Muslims long-term, short-term, or in your own back yard? Contact:

Our Generation Training Center
(770) 456-5881
info@bcwe.org
PO Box 442
Alpharetta, GA 30009

Interested in financially supporting Project North Africa? Make out and send all checks to:

Macedonia World Baptist Missions
PO Box 519
Braselton, GA 30517

Interested in volunteering your summer as an Our Generation Intern? Contact:

Project North Africa
(614) 559-3915
www.projectna.com
tyler@projectna.com

Read more…
www.projectnorthafrica.blogspot.com
www.ladyramblings.blogspot.com
www.luzamusulmanes.blogspot.com
www.cfme.wordpress.com